# DON'T SWEAT THE SMALL STUFF FOR TEENS

Also by the author

*The Big Book of Small Stuff*
*What About the Big Stuff?*
*Don't Sweat the Small Stuff for Men*
*Don't Sweat the Small Stuff in Love* (with Kristine Carlson)
*Don't Sweat the Small Stuff at Work*
*Don't Sweat the Small Stuff with Your Family*
*Don't Sweat the Small Stuff About Money*
*Don't Sweat the Small Stuff . . . and It's All Small Stuff*
*Slowing Down to the Speed of Life* (with Joseph Bailey)
*Handbook for the Heart* (with Benjamin Shield)
*Handbook for the Soul* (with Benjamin Shield)
*Shortcut Through Therapy*
*You Can Feel Good Again*
*You Can Be Happy No Matter What*

# DON'T SWEAT THE SMALL STUFF FOR TEENS

*Simple Ways to Keep Your Cool*

*in Stressful Times*

## RICHARD CARLSON, PH.D.

New York

Library of Congress Cataloging-in-Publication Data

Carlson, Richard.
    Don't sweat the small stuff for teens : simple ways to keep your cool in stressful times / by
    Richard Carlson.—1st. ed.
        p. cm.
    ISBN 0-7868-8597-1
        1. Teenagers—Conduct of life. 2. Stress management for teenagers. I. Title.

BF637.C5 C32 2000
158.1'0835—dc21

00-039655

ISBN-13: 978-0-7868-8597-8

Hyperion books are available for special promotions and premiums. For details contact the
HarperCollins Special Markets Department in the New York office at 212-207-7528, fax
212-207-7222, or email spsales@harpercollins.com.

FIRST EDITION

20   19   18   17   16   15   14   13   12

SUSTAINABLE FORESTRY INITIATIVE
Certified Fiber Sourcing
www.sfiprogram.org

THIS LABEL APPLIES TO TEXT STOCK

This book is dedicated to the present and future teens of the world. May you be happy and live in peace!

# ACKNOWLEDGMENTS

I want to thank all the teens who have written or shared with me over the years. I'd also like to extend a special thanks to my friend and editor, Leslie Wells, and the entire staff at Hyperion. Thanks also to my agents and friends Patti Brietman and Linda Michaels. A special thanks, as well, to my assistant, Nicole Walton, for helping me prioritize and for encouraging me to spend my time focused on this book. Finally, my warmest thanks to my two kids, Jazzy and Kenna, for constantly reminding me what's most important about life. I love you both so much.

# CONTENTS

# INTRODUCTION

I loved being a teen. Then again, sometimes I hated it. I was often enthused but at times apathetic. Occasionally I had vision and a purpose, but other times I was totally confused. Sometimes I was nice, but other times I could be quite selfish, even a real jerk. The first time I fell in love was when I was a teen. That was also the first time I flunked a test. I was a talented athlete but not a great student. At times I was confident, but then again I was embarrassed a lot too. In high school I was so frightened to speak in front of groups that I fainted—twice. I was excited about my future but also a little scared. I was probably a pretty typical teen.

Yet despite the difficulties that I faced, I was always, deep down, a happy person, a natural-born "peacemaker." I cared about the feelings of others and was saddened by cruelty. I loved and appreciated my life, my family, and my friends. For the most part, I stayed out of trouble. I remember wanting to do the right thing. My guess is that a lot of this applies to you too.

Before my teen years were over, I knew I wanted to dedicate my life to the study of happiness, and to help others do the same. In college, I became a "big brother" for the Big Brothers of America program, which was one of the highlights of my young life. That, along with a few other things I was involved in, taught me, beyond any shadow of a doubt, that the best and surest way to become happy and content was by being thoughtful and helpful to others.

Over time, I learned that there were a few other major components to being happy and successful. Much of it is pretty simple. It involves perspective, wisdom, and, most of all, the ability to not be irritated, bothered, and annoyed by the day-to-day things that happen to all of us. In short, the key is to stop sweating the small stuff!

At some point, it became obvious to me (as I'm sure it already is for you) that certain "big stuff" is going to happen to all of us—and that there isn't anything we can really do about it, except, perhaps, to pray for strength and to do our best. Every single one of us experiences loss, difficulties, obstacles, and tragedies. The details will differ, but we all have problems.

And that's precisely why it's so important to learn to stop sweating the small stuff. Life is hard enough when we have to deal with really significant things. But if we can't deal with even the little stuff very well, then we're in for a rocky road. In fact, if we can't learn to stop sweating the small stuff, we're pretty much guaranteed to be stressed out, frustrated, and unhappy much of the time, because either we will be dealing with something really big or we'll be stressing over something fairly small. After all, everything is either one or the other—big or small.

Most people agree that it's pretty tough being a teen. All things considered, however, it's clear to me that it's tougher now than ever. There are the obvious things—drugs, violence, two-income families, dangerous sexual issues, divorce, peer pressure, aggression, and the influence of technology. But there are the less obvious things too—not feeling needed or wanted, mixed messages from parents and society, a ton of negative role models everywhere we look, incredible pressure to perform, self-worth based on accomplishments, and an insecure future, to name just a few.

While learning to stop sweating the small stuff won't make these things go away and won't solve all your problems immediately, it will make dealing with them a little easier. The reason: As you learn to be more accepting of life and as little things don't get to you as much, you will get used to handling things in healthier, easier ways, and with far less struggle. You will become happier, more content and confident, and more at peace with yourself. Consequently, over time, even the big things won't seem quite as bad or as insurmountable.

When we get bent out of shape by little things, when we are irritated at ourselves and others, our (over)reactions not only make us stressed out and miserable, but they actually get in the way of our getting what we want. We lose our bearings, cloud our vision, stumble, and get down on ourselves. We also tend to annoy others who might be in a position to help us or guide us. In short, sweating the small stuff while trying to maneuver through your teens is a huge distraction. It's a little like playing basketball on a slippery ice rink! In other words, your own frustrations and reactions will get in the way of being able to see answers and solutions.

It's understandable why most of us sweat the small stuff. To begin with, we certainly see a lot of others doing it. When we're in the car, for example, and an adult driver is cursing at traffic and clenching his fists, the subtle message is, "If life isn't exactly the way you want it to be, you should become upset." We get tens of thousands of these "Go ahead and sweat the small stuff" lessons when we're kids and while we're growing up. Think back. How many times did someone in that situation say to you, "Don't worry about it. Traffic is simply a part of life. We will get to where we need to go, and we'll probably be on time too"? Probably not very often!

Another example: When someone is criticized, or feels someone doesn't like him or her, the typical response is to become defensive or hurt. Again, how many times when you were growing up did you hear someone, after being criticized, respond by saying, "Criticism is just a way that certain people express themselves. It says less about me than it does about that person's need to criticize me. It's okay, there's no need to take it personally"? In other words, how many people didn't sweat the criticism?

How about when something doesn't go someone's way—she has a minor setback, a traffic ticket, a difference of opinion, or loses her keys? As you know, the typical reaction is to complain, wish that life were different, and feel bad, angry, or ripped off. Have you ever watched adults waiting in line in a grocery store or post office? If so, you'll often see loads of frustration, glaring at watches, and under-the-breath comments. Very seldom do you see people exhibiting great patience in day-to-day living.

Yet can you imagine what your life would be like if you learned to sweat the small stuff even a *little* less often—if these kinds of things, and so many others, simply didn't get to you very much? Can you imagine the edge you'd enjoy in life? No, your life wouldn't be perfect. Yet it would be substantially easier and more manageable. You would get along with others even better than you already do, and your communication skills would improve. You'd feel really good about yourself most of the time, and even when you screwed up, you'd get over it more quickly. Likewise, you'd be more confident because everything wouldn't seem like such a big deal and the stakes wouldn't seem so high. You'd be easier on others too, more patient and forgiving, for example. You'd have more fun too, because your sense of humor would get better, and you'd see the funny side of things. As we learn in the Zen philosophy, when you let go of things rather than struggle against them, your life will begin to flow, and when it does, you'll be on your way to a great life.

There's no question that being around someone who doesn't sweat the small stuff very often (teens or nonteens) is pretty cool and reassuring. And that person can be you. Truthfully, it's not very difficult because all it involves is a little insight, trying a few new things, and looking at stuff a little differently. In fact, it's probably going to be even easier for you than for your parents and other adults because they have far more years of bad habits to overcome. My experience in working with and talking to teens is that you guys pick up on this stuff faster than anyone.

I'm not going to try to lecture you. I don't think you need me to do that. Unlike some people, I don't think the average teen of today is "messed up" anymore than the average teen was back when I was a teen.

Nor am I going to try to be one of you. I'm not. I'm thirty-nine years old and haven't been a teen for almost twenty years. In fact, my daughters will be teens before too long. I'm not going to try to impress you in any way, such as trying to speak or write any differently from the way I usually do. I'm just going to be myself. I've received so much mail over the years from teens that indicate that you're plenty able to read and appreciate my material.

My goal in writing this book is simply to share with you in the same way that I've shared before. My greatest strength is to teach people to be a little happier. I believe that the same types of things that help older people to become happier apply to teens as well.

I hope you'll give these strategies a fair try. I think you're going to like them, and I believe that they can make a difference. I've been blessed with thousands of beautiful letters from teens from all around the world, saying how much learning to stop sweating the small stuff has helped them deal with life more effectively. I hope you will feel the same way. My guess is that as you incorporate these ideas into your life, you will sense a world of difference. Good luck and have fun!

# 1

# DON'T THROW UP
# ON YOUR FRIENDS!

I knew the title of this strategy would grab your attention. In all seriousness, however, if you had a horrible case of the stomach flu, you'd never consider throwing up on your friends. That's obvious.

Yet it's interesting to consider what many of us are tempted to do when we have the emotional equivalent of the stomach flu—when we lose our bearings, fall into a really low mood, and lose it emotionally. Rather than keep our distance, making sure we don't infect others as we would surely do when we have the flu, some of us attack the people we know—friends, parents, and others—with our woes. We share every thought, insecurity, and negative idea that happens to be in our minds.

About once or twice a month, Sam would fall into a horrible mood. He would have what he now calls a "world-class thought attack." During these times his thoughts would become negative, insecure, and pessimistic. He would imagine that his friends were against him, that his parents didn't love him, and that he was doomed to a life of failure. (Who hasn't had thoughts like that while in a low mood?)

Because his thoughts made him feel so bad and seemed so accurate, he would use those occasions to share them with others. He would become angry, defensive, and attacking. He would push people away. It was as if he were throwing up on his friends and on others.

Sam learned that everyone spends a certain amount of time in low moods—that's nothing new. What he learned, however, was that feelings and thoughts are temporary experiences—even the bad ones will lift and go away. When they do, everything will look different, less hostile and frightening. In a low state of mind, everything seems really bad and worse than it probably is. Sam learned that, because low-mood feelings seem so accurate, we're tempted to think we're seeing things the way they really are, even though we aren't. He laughed the first time he realized that, on Monday, for example, he would hate the world, but by Tuesday, everything would seem fine. Wisely, he began to question why he kept getting tricked into believing his "lower" version of reality, even though it always changed.

The trick, he learned, was to treat his low moods as if they were a temporary case of the "emotional flu." In other words, he realized that he only felt this way a few times a month, at most. It became obvious to him that, even though he felt like everyone hated him and that his world was falling apart, it seemed that way only because his mood was so bad. He learned that, generally, it was better to wait it out and confront people when he was feeling better—rather than when he was at his worst. He discovered that in most cases, there was nothing to confront or to be concerned about, after all. And even if there was, it was still better to wait because he would be more himself.

This simple shift in his approach to life changed everything. Now, instead of pushing people away and creating problems for himself, he realizes what's really going on. He's made peace with the fact that, while everyone has low moods, that doesn't mean he has to act on them or even give them so much significance. He's learned that it's okay to ask for help or support and to share with people when he's feeling bad if that seems necessary, but that there's no need to "throw up" on them.

# 2

# CONVINCE YOURSELF THAT ONE
# TEEN DOES MAKE A DIFFERENCE

I was speaking at a bookstore when a teenager in the audience shared the following story about Angela, an eighteen-year-old who was working in an animal shelter as part of a school project. Apparently, the real reason she was working there was that she loved animals.

The purpose of the shelter was to try to find homes for stray and lost dogs and cats. If no home could be found, the animals were destroyed. There were hundreds of animals waiting for homes, and only a small percentage were lucky enough to be adopted.

Angela was known for her willingness to go the extra mile and to work extra hours (without pay) to find homes for the animals.

One day a friend of Angela's came to pick her up at the end of her shift. The two of them were going to a party.

Angela said to her friend, "I have to make one more phone call. There was a woman who came in yesterday who said she might be willing to take Charlie, a sweet older dog who has no other chance. Tomorrow will be his last day here. I have to do something to help him." "Come on, hurry up," said her friend, "we're already late." Angela responded, "Be patient, I have to do this for Charlie."

A few minutes later Angela's friend, who was glaring at her watch, was getting more and more annoyed. Finally she shouted out to Angela, who was still talking on the phone, "Hurry up already. Forget about it. There are too many animals in here for you to make any difference." Just then, her friend overheard Angela on the phone saying "Thank you so much, Mrs. Wright. Sure, I'll meet you down here tomorrow so you can pick up Charlie." As she hung up the phone, she smiled at her friend and said, "Why don't you tell Charlie that I can't make a difference?"

Many teens think that they couldn't possibly make a difference in the world, but that's not so. The honest truth is, you make a difference every time you look the other way when someone makes an innocent mistake, or when you help to make someone's day a little better. You make a difference every time you're thoughtful, helpful, cooperative, generous, compassionate, or kind. Every time you stand up for what's right or allow someone to "be right," you make a difference. The same is true every time you are a good listener or when you offer your forgiveness. Even a simple smile can make a world of difference.

Every time you make an ethical decision, offer your support, choose honesty, or lend a helping hand, you make a difference. Every time you are polite, pick up a piece of litter, or send someone a thankyou note, you make a difference. Angela's kindness wasn't monumental, but it sure made a difference, especially to Charlie. Likewise, your acts matter just as much. Can you imagine what kind of world we would live in if all teens would convince themselves that they too make a difference? That's a world I'd like to live in—and thanks to you, it really can happen!

# 3

# DON'T SWEAT THE BREAKUPS

I hesitated in titling this strategy because I didn't want anyone to think that I was minimizing how difficult it is to break up with a boyfriend or girlfriend. I can assure you, I am not. In fact, I know it's one of the hardest things that a teenager can go through.

I remember the day my first serious girlfriend and first true love broke up with me. I was devastated, and thought I was going to die. I thought I'd never get over it or meet anyone else.

But I did.

In fact, I'm glad. Had it not happened, I wouldn't have married Kris and wouldn't have my kids. The ex-girlfriend is glad too. She's happily married with three beautiful kids of her own. To this day, the two of us are close friends.

The only way that I'm aware of to make breakups more tolerable is to enhance one's perspective and to see that it's necessary. It's weird when you think about it, but if not for breakups, all of us would marry the very first person we were ever interested in! And obviously, in most cases, that's not in our best interests. The truth is, as hard as they can be, breakups are an essential part of life, for all of us.

When you put breakups into this perspective, it's a little easier to spend less energy mourning relationships that are over and, instead, to spend that same energy appreciating them. With appreciation, it's much easier to focus on the gifts of the relationship—the memories, growth, and fun you shared—while at the same time letting go and moving on; realizing that, as painful as it might be, you will love again.

I've found that teens who are able to look at breakups like this are able to maintain a friendship—if not immediately, then at least later on. Rather than being angry that their boyfriend or girlfriend didn't turn out to be "the one," or getting angry, resentful, or wanting revenge because someone changed or didn't live up to their expectations, instead they are able to keep alive a nice feeling for that person and to genuinely wish him or her well.

One of the ultimate tests of being human is to be able to wish someone else well—even when you may be hurt. If you can do this, you'll experience the magic of the healing power of love. You'll notice that you'll bounce back more quickly, feel happier and more self-confident, and even appear more attractive to others when your thoughts and wishes are positive. The love and forgiveness in your heart is more visible to others than any of us can possibly imagine.

So remember, even though it may seem like the end of the world, it probably isn't. It may take awhile, but your breakups usually will end up seeming like a gift in disguise.

# 4

# PRACTICE MENTAL AIKIDO

Years ago I saw a demonstration of the martial art aikido that had a profound and permanent impact on my way of looking at life. Aikido is a gentle-looking but extremely powerful and graceful method of self-defense that takes the physical aggression and strength of your opponent and uses it to your advantage. It has the effect of disarming your opponent with seemingly little effort.

The specific demonstration I witnessed was almost unbelievable. The contest was between two men. The larger man appeared to be at least twice as strong and substantially more angry than the smaller man. The larger man charged his opponent and began swinging his fists. Without so much as blinking an eye, the smaller man calmly reached toward the charging man and moved ever so slightly to one side. To this day I don't know how it happened, but the larger man ended up on the floor, while the smaller man stood above him, not a hair out of place. A similar pattern continued for a few minutes before it became obvious to the stronger man that he had zero possibility of even so much as touching his opponent, much less hurting him. His anger turned to humility as he simply gave up.

I've learned that the emotional equilivent of aikido works wonders in life as well. I've discovered that, more often than not, a gentle approach to resolving conflicts and attacks is most effective. Rather than fighting fire with fire or rolling up my sleeves and fighting back, I attempt to defuse an angry or hostile confrontation with softness and without losing my temper.

Let me give you a practical example. I was being interviewed on a radio talk show when a caller objected to one of my main points. In a somewhat hostile tone, he said some mean things to me, clearly looking for a heated argument. Rather than defend myself or what I had said, I took a deep breath and tried to see his point of view. In a way, I was stepping out of the way of his attack, attempting to defuse his aggression. Then, very gently and with no intended sarcasm, I agreed with him. In fact, I complimented him on his ability to think through his position.

That was it. The argument was over before it had a chance to start. There was nothing left for him to be angry about. Since we were simply expressing our different points of view, it didn't really matter who was right or wrong. And even if he had kept up his hostility, he would have ended up looking pretty bad because I wasn't fighting back.

You probably can imagine how differently the situation would have turned out had I fought back or defended myself. In all likelihood, both of us would have been defensive, an argument would have sprung up, and there would have been no winners, only frustration and unresolved hostility.

It's important to know that mental aikido doesn't necessarily mean you always back down or agree with someone else's point of view. Instead, it involves selecting the perfect peaceful response, whatever that might be. It suggests redirecting negative energy that is headed toward you in a more peaceful way. It might mean that you ask a question, pause, or say nothing at all. It could mean that you ask if you can take the matter up at another time, or say that you'd like to "sit with it" for a moment. The main thrust of mental aikido is that you don't overreact, become overly defensive, yell and scream, or become bothered. You see the situation as a dance, or as an opportunity to resolve your differences peacefully and without drama. Your peace of mind and lack of reaction become your weapons in solving the problem. When you can't be rattled, others will respect you, listen to you, and have a tendency to see things your way.

The same dynamic applies to so many types of potential conflicts and confrontations. Whether it's a friend, parent, someone you're in a relationship with, or even a stranger in the street, mental aikido is a powerful tool in your quest for a more peaceful life. Start working with it today and your conflicts will have less intensity—right away.

# 5

# AVOID THE WORDS "I KNOW" WHEN SOMEONE IS TALKING

If you said to me, "This is what it's like to be a teenager in today's world," and I immediately replied, "Yeah, I know," you'd probably think I was full of it! And you'd be right. Or, if you said, "It's really hard being a teen because . . ." and I chimed back, "I know," you might also think I was misguided, maybe even a little disrespectful. Again, you'd be right.

While there are exceptions, the same applies to many instances where our response is "I know." Many times we really don't "know," we're just saying that we do or assuming that we do. Often our I-know response is offered before the person talking to us is even finished with what he or she had to say. It's a way of cutting someone off, of not having to pay close attention, or of tuning someone out.

When you automatically respond to someone by saying "I know," what you're really saying is, "I'm not listening to you." You're minimizing their comments. It's as if you stop listening because you think you already know all there is to know about something, or you simply don't want to know about something, or you're waiting for your turn to talk, or you're not interested in listening or are unwilling to take the time to listen. Whatever the reason, this response prevents you from hearing things that may be important and drives a deep wedge between yourself and the person you're talking to. Again, how would you feel about me if I responded to each of your statements that way?

I remember a conversation I had with a sixteen-year-old woman and her mother. The teenager asked me, in her mother's presence, if I could make a single suggestion that might possibly improve their relationship. My suggestion was for both of them to eliminate, as best they could, the use of "I know" as a response to the other. The mother had complained that her daughter used this response constantly—especially when she was reminding her daughter of her responsibilities. Likewise, the teen insisted that her mother used this same response many times a day, especially when she was trying to share her feelings with her mom. Both sensed a lack of respect and felt as if they weren't being listened to when this response was used.

According to both people, this single shift in the way they communicated with one another turned out to be a major turning point in their relationship. It encouraged them to listen to each other and learn from one another.

This is one of those strategies that has the potential to show results right away. If you give it a try, you may notice that you have more fun than before when listening to others. You'll hear all of what they have to say instead of the interrupted version. What's more, because you're listening better, the people who talk to you will sense your improved listening skills and will begin to relax around you. Their lack of tension will, in turn, make it easier for you to be around them. As always, good listening skills feed good communication and enhance the quality of your relationships.

One more thing: Once you practice this one for a while, feel free to share this strategy with your mom and dad as well as with other important people in your life who might also benefit from it.

# 6

# CHECK OUT THESE ODDS!
# (THE LIKELIHOOD THAT
# EVERYONE WILL LIKE YOU)

An old friend of mine posed the following question: "If you were fifty feet under water and your snorkel was only one foot long, how often would you be able to breathe?" The answer, of course, is never! It wouldn't matter if you tried ten times, a hundred, or fifty thousand, you'd never be able to breathe.

Similar odds exist for the likelihood that everyone is going to like us! It isn't going to happen. Yet many of us will say or believe things like, "I can't be happy until everyone (or certain people) like me." I think it's critical to ask yourself the philosophical question, "If something is never, ever going to work out, why is the idea still so popular? Why do we continue to pin our hopes and base our happiness on something that is, literally, impossible?" This is a great question because, once you see the odds, you become free from the trap.

Everyone wants to be liked and accepted. I know I do, and I'll bet you do too. Yet, ironically, there is something very reassuring in knowing that there will never be a time when everyone likes us or approves of us. It's nice to know that we're all in the same boat. Regardless of who you are, or what you do, or how popular you become, or how much you try, there will always be people who, for whatever reason, simply don't like you. I've had people not like me because it annoyed them that I seemed happy. Go figure.

There was a time in my life when this would have really bugged or threatened me in some way. I grew up believing that if I was nice to someone, he would naturally be nice to me too. To a large degree, it does work that way.

What I've learned, however, is that while I have a great deal of control over whom I choose to like and how I treat people, I have virtually no control over how others feel about me or how they will treat me.

Here's the good news. I've learned that, while I have no control over who will be nice to me and who will like me, it's *always* the case that the exact people I need in my life will show up and be there for me. There will always be a *perfect* match between my need for acceptance and friendships and the people who accept me and become my friends. It's like a law of nature. I'll always have the perfect set of friends. There is only one condition that is necessary to make this happen.

I will always have the ideal set of friends *as long as* I accept the fact that not everyone I think *should* be my friend will be. That's the important part that will free you from feeling bad when you're not feeling accepted by certain people.

Here's how it works. I'll be nice to someone and hope that a friendship will come about. If the person responds to me in the way I hope, it's great—a friendship is formed. However, if the person doesn't, that's okay too, because it means there isn't a perfect match. And I only want a friendship if it's a perfect match. Do you want friends who don't like you and who won't accept you for who you are? Of course not. Do you want friends who don't really care that much about you, or who think they are doing you a favor by being your friend? No way!

I've decided that I only want friends who genuinely like me for who I am, and vice versa. That's how I know it's a perfect match. The result is that, while I may not have dozens of close friends, the ones I do have are treasured beyond words. To this day, I meet people whom I'd love to be friends with—only they don't seem to feel the same way. It doesn't bother me too much anymore, however, because I've accepted the fact that not all people will feel the way I want them to.

It takes courage to approach friendships and acceptance in this way. However, if you can sense the logic of doing so, you will never again be overly concerned or make your happiness contingent upon certain people liking or accepting you. Since none of us is ever going to get everyone to like or accept us, let's be sure that the friends we do have are a perfect match.

# 7

# GET OUT OF THE
# EMERGENCY LANE

You've undoubtedly heard of the "fast lane." It's that destructive, hyper path that many people turn to for excitement or to fill some void in their life. It's usually associated with a very fast pace, lack of sleep, too many commitments, and too much partying. Those who survive it almost always regret taking it in the first place. It wears you down and makes you feel frazzled.

There's another "lane" to be wary of that I like to call the "emergency lane." This is a less obvious, more socially acceptable lifestyle path that many people find themselves on—often without even knowing it.

In a nutshell, living life in the emergency lane means you treat virtually everything as—you guessed it—an emergency! Every decision seems critical, every mistake is looked at as monumental. There is an almost total lack of perspective. You're usually in a hurry, anxious to get somewhere other than where you are. In a way, it's as if you treat ordinary events like they were front-page news in the newspaper. For example, if I were in the emergency lane and someone criticized me, I'd automatically overreact, as if to say, "RICHARD CARLSON IS CRITICIZED." I'd give the event too much attention, significance, and importance.

The emergency lane is socially acceptable because so many people seem to be in it. When you look around, you'll notice that many people do indeed treat life like an emergency—one drama after another. When you ask someone how she is doing, you'll probably hear, "I'm really busy" as a response. If someone cuts in front of her on the highway, it becomes a federal case in her mind. She discusses the event with others, thinks about how awful it was, and may even try to retaliate with some dangerous driving of her own. If such people have to wait in line, or if something goes wrong, or if someone makes a mistake, or whatever, it's treated as a really big deal and given a great deal of significance.

The reason the emergency lane is so destructive is that inherent in it is dissatisfaction and a great deal of stress. The very fact that you're on edge and in such an enormous hurry means you're stressed out. The fact that everything seems so critical means there's a great deal at stake, a lot on the line. This creates anxiety and fear. You're rarely satisfied because you're keeping track of your own mistakes and those of others. Everything seems to matter.

In addition, when everything is a really big deal to you, it's almost impossible to have any fun. How can you? You're too busy being upset, wishing you were somewhere else, or criticizing life.

I think that the best way out of the emergency lane is to see the humor in it. Try to think about how silly and futile it is to be upset so much of the time. The truth is, I am going to be criticized, and so are you. And we're going to be cut off in traffic and we're going to lose things and make mistakes and our plans are going to be jolted from time to time. But that's life. When you make peace with the fact that life is okay just the way it is, you free yourself from a great deal of frustration.

That doesn't mean we shouldn't do our very best to make things work out the way we would like them to. We certainly should. Yet what's the point in getting uptight and frustrated due to things you have no control over?

The point is, life is just one event after another. It's never going to be perfect, and it's never going to go as smoothly as any of us would like. The nice thing is, as soon as we make peace with these facts, we'll be able to get on with our lives without stressing out over relatively minor things. I hope you'll agree that the emergency lane should be reserved for broken-down autos and that the rest of the time we should steer clear!

# 8

# BE OK WITH YOUR
# BAD HAIR DAY

When I told my daughter that I was going to include this strategy, she was a little irritated at me. She told me that, being a man, I couldn't possibly know what it's like to have a bad hair day. But I do. Unfortunately, I also know what it's like to feel unattractive, overweight, and underdressed. In fact, when I was in Taiwan, I was given the opportunity to meet the president of the country shortly after I arrived. Not only was I jet-lagged from the long flight, but I had forgotten to pack a tie. My eyes were red and I hadn't had a chance to shave. I looked and felt horrible, yet all I could do was laugh at myself.

Obviously, a "bad hair day" isn't usually just about hair, but about the way we look and feel in general. However, having a sense of humor about it has the effect of calming you down and helping you to relax. If, instead of freaking out, you can lighten up a little, usually that will take the edge off of your frustration. This, in turn, will make your bad hair day a little easier to tolerate.

Hair is a funny thing. What's in one year is out the next. What's popular in one culture would look strange in another. Yet while what looks good is arbitrary, we nevertheless take it very seriously. We imagine that other people really care about how our hair looks!

I challenge you, just for fun, to be really honest about the following question. How much time and energy do you spend carefully looking at your friends' hair—or a stranger's hair? Probably not very much. Obviously, you see hair everywhere you look, but do you really study it? And, even if you do, do you give it much thought? Probably not.

The good news is, no one else does either. And even if they did, wouldn't you think their time would be better spent doing something else?

Our bodies are a gift, and it's important to care for them. You also can make a case that it's important to look as nice as we can. Yet in this world of supermodels and slick advertising, it's easy to get sucked into the belief that your hair—and other parts of your body—need to look different from the way they do in order for you to feel good about yourself. Nonsense! That is an attempt to make you feel as if you need something that is being offered—some beauty product, makeup, a certain type of clothing, exercise equipment, or something else. It's sad, but these people actually try to get you to feel bad about yourself, or the way you look, so that you will need them (or their products) to rescue you.

There is a great deal of pressure to look like "him" or "her." The idea, of course, is that you'll feel better if you look like someone else. That's absurd, and has been proven to be inaccurate. If you think about it, it doesn't matter what you look like if you're overly concerned about it. Whether you're sweating the small stuff or sweating the way you look, either way, it translates into unhappiness and stress.

Do you think all supermodels feel great about themselves? Or do you suppose some of them are obsessed about their weight, insecure about the way they look, about getting older, and so forth? Do you think good-looking teenage entertainers who get breast implants or go on crash diets do so because they feel good about themselves, or because they are insecure about their looks? Doesn't it seem that, whatever someone looks like, it never turns out to be good enough? Indeed, the only people who feel good about themselves are those who like and accept themselves just as they are. They take care of themselves and make healthy choices, but they are not obsessed with their looks.

The way to overcome this problem is to see it for what it is—a trap. Once you understand that one of the main reasons you might not feel good enough about yourself is because you are encouraged to feel that way, you'll be able to let go of some of your insecurities. The way to fight back against the pressure to look different is to make the decision to like yourself just the way you are. And, as simplistic as this sounds, once you make this decision, you will feel better about yourself because you're the one making the decision.

As insecure thoughts about your hair and other body parts come to mind, see if you can dismiss them as being insignificant. Remind yourself over and over again that you don't need to be any different in order to like yourself. I'm certain that you have the capacity to see yourself as wonderful and beautiful, just the way you are. I'm also certain that, once you do, you'll find it a whole lot easier to live a happy life.

# 9

# DROP THE DRAMA

This is a fun strategy for me to write about because "drop the drama" is, of course, another way of saying "Don't sweat the small stuff."

I asked Anne, a nineteen-year-old, the following question: "Looking back, what was the hardest 'nonserious' part of being a teen?" After thinking about it for a minute she said, "To me and a lot of my friends, it was probably the drama of daily living." There's no question that the teenage years can be filled with drama. On the other hand, there's also no doubt that making the decision to drop (at least some of) the drama can equate to a much happier and more peaceful life.

The question is, "How do you do that?"

Admittedly, it's a little scary at first, but the only way that I'm aware of is to have the humility to admit that at least a portion of the things that you think of in dramatic terms aren't quite as "life and death" as you sometimes make them out to be. In other words, we often allow ourselves to get all worked up and bothered about things that, on a second look, aren't really that big a deal after all.

A friend, for example, might make a mistake or say something wrong. Rather than forget about it and get on with our day, we allow ourselves to feel offended and annoyed. We think about the mistake during the rest of the day, feeling more and more justified in our irritation.

Many of us might even go home and tell others about it, or call a friend to commiserate, rather than simply letting it go.

These and thousands of other day-to-day incidents (everything from being cut off on the freeway, to having a bad hair day, to making a stupid mistake on a test, to being talked about behind your back, to the phone being out of order, to losing something) can be looked at in one of two ways: as something else to dramatize and get upset over, or as yet another chance to let something go. And while it can be really tempting to blow these types of things out of proportion, it's ultimately better for your sanity, your friendships, and your happiness to learn to let them go.

The problem with sweating the small stuff is that there is, and always will be, an endless supply of things to sweat over. There always will be friends making mistakes, strangers cutting us off, things being lost, plans going astray, and all the rest. Pretty soon we're sweating everything, and life seems to be one drama right after another. Needless to say, this takes an enormous amount of mental energy and saps the joy from your life.

As you learn to let some of these things go, however, you'll find yourself experiencing far less stress and aggravation. You'll be left with more mental energy and creativity in order to live life to its fullest.

# 10

# GET HIGH!

No, not like that!

Better yet, there is a safe, nonaddictive, healthy, peaceful, legal, and free way to experience a *natural* high. It's called meditation. And once you've experienced it, anything that is self-destructive will become far less appealing to you. Meditation is not only peaceful, it also contributes to clarity, happiness, even productivity. I often get my best ideas right after I finish meditating. My mind is clear and ideas seem to come to me almost out of the blue.

Tens of millions of people around the world use meditation on a daily basis. There are many different varieties of meditation, but, in a nutshell, it's a simple procedure that involves an attempt to clear your mind and relax. It takes anywhere from five to twenty minutes (or longer), and, ideally, it's done every day.

Although I practice meditation regularly, I'm by no means an expert. The truth is, it's more difficult than it sounds. As you sit down, close your eyes and attempt to quiet your mind. You may be surprised to discover that your mind is extremely busy and active. Yet with practice, it's possible to learn to experience an inner stillness that makes you feel peaceful, joyful, enthusiastic, and loving. And when you feel this way, your entire life will be easier and less stressful. You'll get along with people better, act more loving, and, without question, sweat the small stuff less often!

If you're at all open to learning meditation, I suggest you take a class or read a book on the subject. Go to the library or your favorite bookstore to find out more. Or even do some research on the Web. There is plenty of great information out there. Some of my favorite authors who have written on the subject include Stephen Levine, Jack Kornfield, and Thich Nhat Hanh, to name just a few.

If one of your goals is to be happier, meditation may be for you. I hope you'll take some time to check it out.

# 11

# TRY NOT TO BECOME
# A FAULT-FINDER

One of the easiest things in the world is to become a fault-finder. As the name suggests, this is the almost universal tendency to be on the lookout, thinking about, and constantly pointing out the flaws and imperfections of yourself, others, society, and the world. Because our natural tendency is to want things to improve, and since there is so much in the world that obviously needs improving, it's no wonder that so many of us fall into the habit.

The problem with being a fault-finder, especially a really good one, is that it's an almost guaranteed way to keep yourself unhappy, stressed out, and frustrated. When your mind is primarily directed toward problems, pitfalls, and imperfections, that's exactly what you'll see. Over time you'll become even more discriminating until, at some point, you'll become an expert.

A few years ago I received a letter from seventeen-year-old Kerry, who described herself as a world-class fault-finder, almost always bothered by things. People were always doing things that annoyed her, and nothing was ever good enough. She was highly self-critical and also found fault with her friends. She became a real sourpuss, a drag to be around.

Unfortunately, it took a horrible accident to change her attitude.

Her best friend was hurt very badly in a car wreck. What made it almost impossible to deal with was that the day before the accident, Kerry had visited her friend and had spent the whole time criticizing her choice of boyfriends, the way she was living, the way she related to her mother, and various other things she felt she needed to express. It wasn't until her friend was badly hurt that Kerry realized that she had made a habit of finding fault. Very quickly, Kerry learned to appreciate life (including the imperfections) rather than to judge everything so harshly. She was able to extend her new wisdom to other parts of her life as well.

Perhaps most of us aren't as extreme at our fault-finding skills, but when we're honest, we can be pretty darn critical of the world. I'm not suggesting you ignore problems, or that you pretend that things are better than they are, but simply that you learn to allow things to be as they are—at least most of the time, and especially when it's not a really big deal. Otherwise, what happens is that the habit of pointing out what's wrong becomes a mind-set, a way of seeing the world so that your life becomes mostly about observing and pointing out the imperfections of others and what needs to be improved. This, of course, more than anything will encourage you to sweat the small stuff.

On the other hand, if you can train yourself to "bite your tongue" when you see minor imperfections, or people making mistakes, and so forth, you'll be, in effect, training yourself *not* to sweat the small stuff. With a little practice, you'll get really good at letting things go, even things that used to bug you or irritate you. And when you do, you'll get back your enthusiasm and zest for life—because life is awesome when you're not busy finding fault with it.

# 12

# LET HIM HAVE HIS ACCIDENT
# SOMEWHERE ELSE

When I was thirteen years old, my parents took me to a seminar that was designed to help people learn more perspective. I remember only one thing from that seminar—but that one thing has stuck with me like gum on my shoes. It's helped me, virtually every day, since that time.

The man doing the teaching was talking about how irritating and frustrating it can be when you're driving and people come up too fast behind you. They tailgate you and might even flash their lights. In some instances, they even honk their horn or flip you off. We're talking about real jerks.

The instructor asked the question, "What can you do in a situation like this?" People in the audience offered a variety of vindictive solutions, such as "Slam on your brakes," "Turn on your tail lights so the driver will think you're slamming on your brakes," "Slow down to annoy him," and "Flip him off too."

His response is the insight that I've never forgotten. He said in a calm voice, "Why not simply stay calm, pull over, and let him go have his accident somewhere else?" What a brilliant suggestion. Think about it. It's virtually guaranteed that someone that angry and aggressive is going to have an accident. Why would you want to be involved? Why would you want anything to do with someone like that?

In this day and age of road rage, this strategy is particularly important. Fighting back can only make matters worse and escalate an already dangerous situation. I drive quite a bit and have implemented this strategy dozens of times over the years. And to this day, it's never failed me. The jerks behind me always whiz by and are out of my life forever. What could be easier?

Learning to stop sweating the small stuff involves deciding what things to engage and what things to ignore. It's important to know when to pursue something and when to back off. In this case, you're not backing off as much as you are pulling over. In any event, you'll be glad you did.

# 13

# BE SELECTIVE WHEN
# CHOOSING YOUR BATTLES

Everyone has battles to fight. I'm supposed to be the champion of not sweating the small stuff, yet battles come up all the time in my life too. The differences between people and the way we all see and interpret things—as well as some of the inherent facts of life (e.g., two people who disagree can't both get their way) make this a virtual certainty, an unavoidable and unpleasant part of life.

It seems to me that the question isn't whether you're going to have to fight battles in your life; you will. The more important question is, "Which battles do you choose to fight?"

You've probably known people who rarely let things go, those who seem to battle over practically anything—correcting people, arguing, proving themselves, pointing out flaws, needing to be right all the time, validating their sense of worth, complaining and whining, and so forth. The tiniest dispute or disagreement becomes an automatic battle.

The problem with living this way is twofold. First, it's exhausting. When everything is seen as a big deal and worth fighting over, your whole life becomes a battleground. And who needs that? Second, people will begin to push you away and/or avoid being around you. After all, who wants to be around someone who is argumentative and conflict-oriented—someone who can rarely just let things go? Further, when you fight battles all the time, no one will take you very seriously; they will assume you're just letting off steam.

Sara, a thirteen-year-old, shared with me the following idea: She said that she used to be the kind of person who would battle over practically anything until she realized that she was spending too much of her life fighting battles. She started doing something that has worked really well for me too. Whenever a conflict came up—a potential argument, disagreement, or whatever—she asked herself to rate the importance of the potential battle on a scale of 1 to 10 (low to high). For example, if she and her sister were about to battle over who forgot to put away the hairbrush, she might rate that a #1. A negotiation with her parents about what time she needed to be home from her friend's house might be a #5; her teacher accusing her of cheating might be a #9 or even a #10.

She decided that she would choose *not* to do battle over anything that rated less than a #5. And, she added, "Even a 5 or 6 is questionable." Instead, she would find a way to simply let it go, or find a way to peacefully resolve the issue without needing to be "right." You can imagine that the number of conflicts she has to deal with has been dramatically reduced. She now has more time to do the things she enjoys.

What's interesting is that practically everyone who explores this strategy quickly discovers that the battles they do choose to fight are easier to win. When you battle less often, you are more focused on your positions—and other people take your positions far more seriously.

The trick, of course, is to rate the importance of any particular potential battle appropriately. It's easy to justify rating something too high, especially when you're angry or frustrated. So, try to keep your ratings as low as possible. My own rule of thumb is this: When in doubt, I assume I'm probably rating something too high. I try to find ways to keep my ratings low, knowing that the fewer battles I fight, the happier and more relaxed I remain. Sara and I have learned the same lesson. Some battles are worth fighting—but not very many. I hope this becomes true for you as well.

# 14

# MAKE PEACE WITH
# YOUR MISTAKES

One of the most powerful and inspirational spiritual awakenings and a sure-fire way to become happier is to make peace with your mistakes. I'm not talking about paying lip service to this wisdom by saying, "Sure, I know—everyone makes mistakes," but instead by genuinely making peace with the fact that mistakes are not only inevitable but important.

I read about a Zen master who described life as "one mistake after another." And, if you think about it, he was right. From a certain perspective, life can be described as a series of mistakes, one right after another, with a little space in between. We mess up, make amends, and change. We then go on with our life. Sooner or later we make another mistake, learn from it, make the necessary adjustments, and move on. The mistakes offer us the continual opportunity to learn and evolve. Without them, there would be no growth, no reason to change. Accepting this idea makes it much easier to forgive ourselves and others when we (or they) "mess up." It's almost impossible to be too hard on yourself (or anyone else) when you see the importance of mistakes in the bigger scheme of things.

Obviously, this isn't to say we make mistakes on purpose or that we don't do our best to avoid them—that would be ridiculous. Nor does it suggest that we condone or enjoy the mistakes of others. We don't.

What I am suggesting, however, is that mistakes are the way we learn to make allowances in our thinking and behavior; they are the things that encourage us to change direction and to grow as human beings.

Think of the world's best athletes. I was watching Andre Agassi, one of the top tennis players in the world, play a match. It made me feel better about my game when I realized that even the world's best players make plenty of mistakes. I read somewhere that the baseball great Babe Ruth struck out twice for every home run that he hit. That really puts mistakes into perspective.

When I was fourteen years old, I was talking behind someone else's back to a mutual friend. I was being mean-spirited and spreading a vicious rumor. I didn't know it, but the person I was bad-mouthing was standing right behind me and heard everything I said. He was crushed, and I was embarrassed. This was a mistake I've never forgotten.

This mistake, however, was one of thousands that I made that helped me to become the person I am today. I learned more from that mistake than I could have learned in any class, lecture, or book. It hit me hard where it counts—in my heart. I didn't enjoy it, I'm not proud of it, but, boy, did I learn from it. I'm a kinder person today because of it.

Everyone makes mistakes, big ones and small ones. If you can see your mistakes as a means to help you become a better person and to make better decisions, you'll be able to be easier on yourself and get through difficult times much easier. In the long run, you'll make fewer mistakes. And if people have made mistakes that have hurt you or affected you negatively, you can apply this same philosophy to help you forgive those people so that you can move forward with greater ease and confidence.

# 15

# BE HAPPY FOR OTHERS

I love this strategy because it's one of the easiest and surest ways to reduce your stress and become a happier person. It's also a way that you can be of service to others. Anyone can do it, and all it takes is a slight shift in attitude.

It's very seductive to get into what I like to call "the envy habit." Even though it's hard to admit, it's tempting to be a little jealous or envious when someone you know is experiencing joy or success.

Nineteen-year-old Diane confessed that when her best friend, Denise, had fallen in love, she was "green with envy." Denise was totally happy. And although Diane had told Denise she was "so happy for her," she was having thoughts like, "How come that didn't happen to me?"

When you take a step back and look at this typical reaction more carefully, it's easy to see that the person hurt by this reaction is Diane. Her failure to be genuinely happy for her friend interferes with her own ability to be happy. It limits her own joy by keeping her focused on her own wants, needs, and desires.

When you wish others well, however, and share in their happiness, *you* get to experience their happiness with them. In a predictable and reliable way, your mental enthusiasm translates into feelings of inner happiness.

Whether your friend made the team and you didn't, or whether someone you know got into a certain college or made an A on an exam or got a great job that you would love to have yourself, it's all the same. Whenever you make the conscious choice to share in the happiness of others, you are guaranteeing a certain amount of joy for yourself.

Have you ever been really excited about something and shared it with someone who said, "That's great," but you know he didn't really mean it? It's a very deflating experience that takes some of the thrill away from the person doing the sharing. It sure doesn't make you want to tell him the next time something happens.

I'll bet you'll agree that one of the greatest joys in the world is being able to share your happiness or success with someone else—and having that person be as happy for you as you are. My friend Benjamin is like that. Whenever I'm happy about something, I can't wait to share it with him because, every single time I do, it's almost like he's the one having my experience! He's thrilled for me—and "all ears," listening to every part of the story. My joy is his joy. It's one of the things I love most about him. My goal is to be that kind of friend too.

There's no specific way to do this. All you have to do is agree that being happy for others is important and in your best interest. Then you simply make the choice to be genuinely happy for others when they are happy, experiencing good fortune, or have achieved something they are proud of. If you extend this philosophy to your friends, parents, siblings, and others, you'll be enhancing your joy, being a great friend (and daughter or son), and helping to spread happiness on Earth. You'll be part of the solution in the creation of a kinder and gentler world.

# 16

# VOLUNTEER YOUR TIME

A staggering number of teens are now volunteering their time to help others or some selected cause. There are several reasons for this encouraging trend.

First of all, it's now widely understood that teens can and do make a difference. Your commitment to doing helpful things for others really counts and it really helps. You have much-needed energy, vitality, and enthusiasm.

Second, volunteering your time for others, or to a cause you love, helps you as much as it helps the person or cause you are helping! I'm not kidding, and I'm not exaggerating. There is something inherent in service work that is so gratifying it actually reduces your stress and makes you happier. Indeed, one of the best and quickest ways to help yourself is to help others. To be honest, I've never met a person out there helping others who didn't agree. Many people—including teens—have told me that volunteering their time is the most valued part of their routine.

Many cities have volunteer centers where you can learn how you can help, or you can find books on volunteerism in the library or bookstore. There are dozens of possibilities. You can help younger kids learn to read, or spend time keeping lonely people company. You can do important work for the homeless or for people who are hungry. You can work with animals or the environment. The list goes on and on.

It's really fun to get involved and help others. And if you don't want it to be a formal commitment, there are things you can do on your own. My daughter Kenna is committed to helping keep litter off the streets. She and I both have a minimum number of pieces of trash we pick up each day. It's not big deal, but it makes a difference. If you pick up 10 pieces of trash a day, that's 3,650 pieces a year. If everyone did that, there wouldn't be as much litter on the streets. She's also a vegetarian because she loves animals and doesn't want to eat them. These are two ways she has decided to help.

The point is, you can do anything, and it doesn't have to take a lot of time. An hour a week makes a world of difference; even an hour a month is worth doing. If every teen in the world donated one hour each month to a good cause of his or her choice, the world would be a much nicer place to live in.

Volunteering is something you can do with your friends. What a great way to spend some time together, having fun and being helpful to important causes. If you do this, you'll be proud of yourself for making a difference, and you'll be helping your community become a better place.

# 17

# CHECK OUT THE SPACE BETWEEN YOUR THOUGHTS

The first time someone suggested this to me, I thought they were absolutely nuts. Once I took a moment to consider the suggestion, however, I was able to see what was being said. Today, many years later, I use this strategy on a regular basis—without even thinking about it.

If you were to speak a sentence right now, and then another, you might notice a tiny pause between them. It might only be a millisecond. Tinier still, almost minuscule, is a space between individual thoughts. You almost have to imagine it to experience it.

This tiny little space is often the key to taking the "high road" instead of the "low road."

Have you ever had the experience of being just about ready (on the edge) of making a decision, or doing something, but then, at the very last instant, you decided against it? If so, you've experienced the space between your thoughts. There was a very tiny moment of space—a moment of quiet—that allowed you to see the fork in the road. In a split second, you saw another option, or had an insight or a change of heart. You saw that you could go in a new direction. If you were barreling forward, full speed ahead in your thinking, and there were absolutely no spaces between those thoughts, it would be difficult to change gears or see another way. It would be like a train out of control. But with that little tiny bit of space, you have the possibility to see something new.

Sometimes when someone is critical of me, I start to get upset and think defensively. Then, just when I'm about to say something hurtful back to them, I see that I have a choice. Instead of retaliating, I'll simply let it go. It's that moment of clarity.

I've had teens tell me stories about how they were "just about" to go along with the crowd and participate in something they knew in their heart was wrong. They may have been on the phone with a friend, discussing the time and place, when, right before they agreed, they had one of those moments and said, instead, "I'm sorry, I can't do it."

To benefit from the space between your thoughts, you don't have to do anything different from what you're already doing. All you really have to do is be open to the possibility that the spaces are there—and begin to look for them. If you don't notice them, don't worry about it. Just be open.

You do this because in those spaces lie clarity and wisdom. It's most helpful to be looking for these spaces whenever you're really upset about something. The simple act of looking slows down your thinking ever so slightly and can break a negative or potentially self-destructing train of thought.

# 18

# ASK A TRUSTED FRIEND
# OR FAMILY MEMBER,
# "WHAT ARE MY WEAKNESSES?"

For most people, this is such a hard thing to do that I hesitated to include it in this book. However, the rewards are potentially so great for those brave enough to try it that I decided it was worth it.

As you know, our trusted friends and certain family members know us better than anyone else. They see us at our best—and they see us at our worst. Sometimes it seems they know us as well or better than we know ourselves. They are aware of our strengths as well as our weaknesses. They see us shine, and they see us getting in our own way.

Often there is a fine line between the life we have and the life we want. The problem is, it's really hard to see the ways that we can sometimes get in our own way. All of us have blind spots about our own attitudes, behaviors, and ways of being, and, to one degree or another, we become stuck in our ways. Our habits become invisible to us.

And while, deep down, it's easy to see that our friends and family members might be able to help us see things about ourselves, ways that we might change to improve our lives, it's nevertheless hard to ask for any sort of help. We are usually too proud, embarrassed, or defensive to find out what they might say. It might hurt our feelings, make us angry, or force us to look in the mirror and admit that they are right.

Remember, however, that there is a big difference between having a friend blurt out to us, "You should stop doing that—it's wrecking your life," versus us asking a friend for a guidance or some type of suggestion. This exercise is not about asking a question like, "Hey, what do you think I should do in this situation?" but rather something much deeper, such as, "Do you see any ways that I get in my own way, or things that I do that are self-destructive?"

I've asked my best friends for this type of advice dozens of times over the years, and each time it has been incredibly helpful. I've had friends tell me that I was too speeded up, that I talked too much, that I needed to become a better listener, to name just a few. Every single time I've asked, the person was right on the money. And, each time, it helped me to change for the better.

Rachel and Vicky, both seventeen years old, had been best friends for five years. Vicky was frustrated and down on herself because guys didn't seem to like her very much. She gathered the courage to ask Rachel if she knew what was going on. Rachel was hesitant to say anything, knowing that what she had to say might hurt her friend's feelings. Vicky said, "Just tell me, I can handle it." Rachel told her that when she (Vicky) was nervous, she would always talk about nothing but herself. She would never ask questions or express any interest whatsoever in the guy she was talking to.

Because she was the one who initiated the question, Vicky was able to handle it and, in fact, learned a great deal from it. She was able to make the necessary changes in her behavior to solve her problem with the guys she would meet.

The only way this strategy works is if you decide in advance that you're going to listen to what is said and not be defensive. You must approach this exercise as a genuine learning experience, a chance to see something new about yourself or your behavior. You don't necessarily have to accept or take action upon what is said, but you must make a genuine effort to take the advice to heart.

This strategy is one of the key ways I have been able to grow and develop as a human being. I'm sure if you give this a try, the same might be true for you.

# 19

# ROOT FOR THE UNDERDOG

I've been a San Francisco 49ers football fan for many years. And why not? After all, the 49ers were arguably the best team of the 1990s, winning several Super Bowls and always being competitive. But in 1999, it was a little tougher. The team lost twelve of its sixteen games! I learned that the measure of a good fan isn't whether you can cheer for your team when it is on top—that's easy. No, the true measure of a good fan is whether you can continue to root for your team when it's down, or losing.

In the same way, it's easy to root for popular people, those on top. Anyone can do that. It makes you feel like you fit in and are going along with the crowd. When you cheer for, are respectful of, and are nice to popular people, no one questions your motives. You don't have to take a stand against anyone; nor do you risk your own popularity.

Indeed, the true measure of how kind you are as a human being isn't whether you can be friendly to your existing friends and those who are already popular—that's easy—but whether you can be nice to other people too.

It can be a little tougher to root for someone who isn't as popular or someone who is a little different or who doesn't have as many friends. To do so could mean that you're breaking free from a group or risking disapproval from your existing friends. On a very superficial level, rooting for the underdog appears to be risky.

If you reflect for a moment, however, on the upside of rooting for the underdog, I think you'll agree that the benefits far exceed the risks. Many teens have shared with me that reaching out to someone a little less popular, or new to their school or group of kids, had earned them the best friend they've ever had. In other words, the person they reached out to (the underdog) appreciated their effort and became a very loyal and trusted friend. The fact that people aren't yet "popular" has nothing whatsoever to do with whether they are nice people who would make great friends.

When you reach out to someone, particularly someone who doesn't have a million friends or who might be a little lonely, it demonstrates that you are a kind person who sees beyond what's "in" at the moment. It's a way of contributing to the world—making it just a little bit friendlier. Reaching out makes the other person feel good and does the same for you too. In my entire lifetime, I've never heard of anyone saying, "I'm really upset because I was nice to that person who needed someone to be nice to them." On the other hand, hundreds of people have told me that being nice to people who need friends has brought them a great deal of personal joy and satisfaction.

Rooting for the underdog *doesn't* mean you feel sorry for the person. It simply means that you recognize that the person hasn't yet been blessed—as you already might have been—with the approval, acknowledgment, and friendship of others.

In no way am I suggesting that you stop being nice to popular people; you can do that too. I'm only suggesting that you open your heart and widen your circle to include others as well. In doing so, you'll make those people happy, set an important example for others, and feel good about yourself. What a great way to make this world an even better place.

## 20

# MAKE PEACE WITH BOREDOM

I thought the title of this strategy might get your attention! No one likes to be bored, and we live in a time when boredom is often seen as completely unacceptable. Most people can't stand it—even for a moment. Something has to be going on, or turned on, or being planned. There must be some type of stimulus going on every waking moment. We're spending time with someone else on the phone or on the Internet, or we're watching television. Many people have cell phones so as not to lose touch while away from home, and radios in the shower so as not to experience silence. It seems to me that people often define a good life as being a series of stimulating activities, one right after another, with the goal of having as little space in between as possible.

Unfortunately, the only way out of this frenetic maze is to see it as a trap. There is nothing wrong with computers or cell phones, or television or beepers, or game machines or fax machines, or any of the rest of it. Yet if you are dependent on ongoing stimulation, you actually set yourself up to be bored a great deal of the time. Think about it for a moment. What happens to most people you know when there is nothing going on? Anxiety, boredom, or some degree of lack of satisfaction? But the conclusion most people come to is that the solution is to be sure you never, ever, have nothing going on.

When you are overstimulated, your mind keeps looking for more, more, more. There is constant pressure to always be entertained and busy. The ante keeps rising so that it takes more and more to keep you satisfied.

Fifteen-year-old Robert started out with a video game he loved to play on his television set in his spare time. Pretty soon he needed more games; better ones with more action. When he'd mastered the games, he needed to have one with him all the time so he wouldn't be bored. He was able to get a hand-held version, which solved his boredom for a very brief time. He learned to play it while at school in such a way that no one could see him doing it. Now he plays while the television is on, and his parents have trouble getting him to turn it off during dinner. He carries it with him on his way upstairs to use his computer, which he is on several hours a day, playing games and chatting with others. He loves the phone too, and stays in close touch with his buddies, who all do the same thing with their time.

At some point Robert started getting into trouble because he thought it was fun. It was stimulating. He needed more action, more things to do. If Robert was alone on a beach, he wouldn't know what to do. He'd be bored stiff. If he was sitting next to a running river, he'd be bored too. His inner creativity had disappeared, replaced by an obsession with outer activities.

I'm not bashing or blaming technology. I'm only suggesting that when you decide that it's okay if something isn't going on all the time, you train your mind to be more easily satisfied, which always translates into happiness and joy. Very quickly, you'll learn to feel more peaceful.

When you're peaceful, you can have fun on a computer, at an amusement park, or while you're all alone, sitting on a bench. You'll be free.

Practice having a little space in between activities. If you can learn to sit still with nothing going on, even for a few minutes at a time, you'll be way ahead of the game. You'll not only become happier, but you'll actually enjoy the things you already spend time doing much more. You'll feel a sense of relief, as if you're off the hook.

Making peace with boredom doesn't mean you stop doing things or that you seek out boredom. It also doesn't mean you stop achieving or winning. It simply means that you become comfortable with a little space and a little silence.

# 21

# DON'T LET YOUR
# LOW MOODS TRICK YOU

In my opinion, one of the most important ingredients of a happy, fulfilled, and successful life is an understanding of moods. Without it, you're almost sure to experience a great deal of frustration, stress, and anxiety. At times, you'll probably be deceived into believing that your life and what you're experiencing is even harder than it actually is, and you'll probably make a bigger deal out of things than you really need to. In other words, you'll be sweating the small stuff, often. By learning about your moods, however, you can protect yourself, to a large degree, from the illusions your mind can create when you're in a really bad mood. You'll be able to let go of things much easier, know when to back off, keep your sense of humor, and get along better with everyone, especially yourself. In short, you'll save yourself from a ton of grief and your life will become much easier.

Think about how powerful and deceptive your moods can be. Most teens have told me that when their mood is good, they feel secure that, for the most part, they enjoy their life. They are confident, responsible, reasonably happy, optimistic, and inwardly secure. They like their friends and themselves, and even Mom and Dad are pretty cool! When they think about a problem, while in a good mood, they feel relatively confident that they can solve it. When they think about school, that's okay too. When someone says something mean, and you're in a good mood, you may not like it very much, but you probably can handle it because you are patient and have at least some perspective about things.

However, think about how you experience these *exact* same things when your mood is low, when you're feeling insecure, depressed, angry, or frightened. Your life can seem unbearable, and everywhere you look, you see stress. You probably don't like yourself as much as you do when your mood is higher—or your friends or your parents or your teachers or anyone else. You tend to take things personally, and you don't like the way you look. You might even become more critical of others when your mood is low. School can seem like a drag, and even relatively small problems can seem insurmountable. You probably sweat the small stuff.

And what's strange is that your feelings in a low mood seem so accurate and realistic, as if what you're seeing and feeling is the way things really are. We're all like this.

But wait a minute! What does this tell you? The *exact* same life and the *exact* same set of circumstances—the same problems, challenges, body, parents, schoolwork, hassles, teachers, siblings, and so forth— seem very different depending on how you are feeling. In other words, when you're feeling "off" or low, it taints your view of everything you see and the way you experience everything in your life. It usually makes things seem worse than they really are. In lower moods, you'll always be more reactive, pessimistic, and negative. You'll take things more personally and will get frustrated more easily.

What a great thing to know! Can you imagine how much easier your life will be and how many arguments, conflicts, and problems you can avoid when you don't take your low moods so seriously—and when you don't take the thoughts you have during those low moods so seriously? When you recognize that you're not seeing things correctly in that moment? I'm not saying you don't have real problems; you do. I'm simply saying that you'll relate to those problems very differently depending on what mood you're in. And knowing that is a huge relief.

Here's the trick. When you're feeling low (down, angry, not yourself, serious, frightened, or whatever), rather than trust what you are seeing and feeling, and taking it too seriously and reacting to it, see if you can become just a little suspicious of the way you're seeing things. Rather than blaming yourself, or others, or your circumstances, or your life for the way you're feeling, put at least some of the blame where it belongs—on your mood! Remember, if you were in a better mood, you would be looking at the same things very differently.

Rather than saying, "I hate my life," say to yourself, "Of course it seems like I hate my life—my mood is really low right now. I'm always more negative about everything when I'm in a bad mood. But I know I won't feel this way when my mood goes back up." The idea is to be as graceful and patient as possible when your mood is low. Try not to overreact, make important decisions, solve your problems, figure out your life, or argue when you're feeling low, because you won't have much common sense, compassion, or wisdom.

It's hard because, when you're feeling low, that's exactly when you're going to *want* to try to figure everything out because that's when things seem so urgent and important. But if you can be patient when you're low and try not to overreact or panic, in many instances your mood will start to change, perhaps even go back up on its own. And, as it does, everything will look a lot better. Exercising patience takes a little practice, but it's worth it.

# 22

# DON'T LET THE LOW MOODS OF
# OTHERS TRICK YOU EITHER

Everyone has low moods. I do, and you do. So do your friends, teachers, siblings, parents, relatives, neighbors, strangers, and everyone else.

And although we all experience our low moods a little differently, to some degree, the way people *act* in lower moods is quite predictable. A vast majority of people, in low moods, will be at least somewhat negative, reactive, pessimistic, and argumentative. Low moods will bring out cynicism, anger, frustration, and stress. In those low moods, people will tend to be critical and defensive, and they might even say and do mean things. They will tend to have poor judgment and will lack patience.

Think about it. Have you ever met anyone whom you absolutely love to be around while she is in a sour mood? No way!

Here's what's incredibly useful to know. When someone you know or love is in a low mood, he will say and do things that would never occur to him if his mood was higher. A very powerful negative cloud overcomes his perspective. A vast majority of people will react to their low moods as if what they are experiencing is the way they really feel. In other words, they won't realize they are in a bad mood and that their mood is tainting their view of things. Instead, they will overreact, say mean things, blame others, freak out, panic, get bossy or critical, or whatever, and they will have absolutely no idea that their mood is dictating their negative behavior. It's strange because an hour later, they will probably feel very differently.

This is one of the weird laws of being human: Low moods trick all of us. And it doesn't matter if it's your best friend, a boyfriend or girlfriend, a teacher, one of your parents, or whomever—none of us is exempt. I guarantee you that you wouldn't like me when I'm in a really bad mood!

Here's the point. Once you start to recognize the deceptive power of moods, it's easy to begin taking them less personally; you see them for what they are. You start to realize that people (all of us), literally, can't help it! We aren't trying to be reactive and critical, it just happens. It's almost like being drugged and not knowing that you've been drugged. Because you understand what's going on, you begin to make allowances for the fact that everyone acts strangely in low moods and that it really isn't personal.

Here's a good example. I heard a story about a seventeen-year-old woman named Janie who had just learned about moods by reading one of my books. She had told someone that in her seventeen years of living, *nothing* had been so instantly useful in terms of helping her relationships. In fact, what she had learned was "like magic."

Here's what happened, as it was told to me: Janie's best friend had snapped at her and said something terribly mean. She had exploded at Janie and said she didn't want to be friends anymore. Rather than take her words too personally, as she would certainly have done in the past, Janie realized that her friend was in a really bad place emotionally. She decided not to react, argue back, or even defend herself. She knew her friend was in such a negative place, she couldn't possibly be receptive to anything Janie had to say.

Instead, she waited a day and then dropped by her friend's house to see if she wanted to talk. Her friend opened the door and immediately gave her an enormous hug and told her how much she loved her. Sobbing, she apologized, and the two of them had a very healing, heart-to-heart talk. The problem was solved rather than exacerbated and made into a federal case simply because Janie understood what was happening inside her friend.

This doesn't mean you excuse everything that people say and do in low moods, that you don't hold them accountable, or that you allow anyone to walk over you. It only suggests that often, when someone is saying or doing something that you don't like or approve of, it has nothing whatsoever to do with you but everything to do with the person's own state of mind. In many instances, simply knowing this allows you to see what's really going on so that you don't take it personally and feel hurt, betrayed, or annoyed. All you're really doing is making allowances for the fact that people aren't themselves when they are in bad moods. You still won't like the way people act when they are low, but when you understand why they're acting this way, it makes them much easier to deal with.

Janie mentioned that all her relationships had become better by virtue of her new understanding of moods. I hope that you will be affected in a similar way. Remember, whether it's your own low mood, or someone else's, take it with a grain of salt. It probably will pass if you leave it alone.

## 23

# SEE YOUR CHOICES
# AS FORKS IN THE ROAD

When you think back a few years, it's usually pretty easy to see that each of the major choices you made can be seen as forks in the road. In other words, you made a decision or choice that led you in a certain direction. Had you made a different choice, you would, in all likelihood, have gone in a different direction.

For example, you may have stood up for someone who was being picked on in front of others. That choice may have brought the two of you closer together as friends. Had you joined in on the taunting, you may not have been friends today. That single decision made a world of difference. Or perhaps you made the choice to skip a party or something else you really wanted to do so that you could study just a little bit more for a test. As it turned out, that tiny bit of extra effort on your part pushed you over the top and opened new doors. Had you gone to the party instead, you may have had more fun, but probably wouldn't have done so well. You can probably think of tons of similar types of examples.

Natalie, a seventeen-year-old, shared with me that one of the most important forks in the road she remembers is when she withstood the peer pressure and made the conscious decision not to begin drinking or smoking. She said that there is no question that this single choice, which wasn't easy for her to make, led her to hanging out with her current group of friends who have been her lifeline. She believes that had she made the choice to go ahead and smoke or drink (or both), it would have resulted in a whole different set of friends and a whole different set of experiences. Again, a single decision or choice makes a world of difference—a different fork in the road.

Sometimes it's difficult to know when you're at a fork in the road. A good rule of thumb is that forks often occur when you're uneasy about a choice you're considering, or when your conscience is speaking to you. How many times have you heard stories about teens who make only one mistake—but it's a big one? You hear them say after the fact, "I knew I shouldn't have done it, but I didn't listen to my intuition." But by then they were in jail or on drugs, or had become pregnant or gotten someone else pregnant, or something like that.

Seeing your choices as forks in the road is very empowering and reassuring. Doing so enables you to take charge of your life and helps you realize that it's never too late to change direction. Since every choice is a fork in the road, each decision brings with it new hope and promise. The decision to put more effort into school, sports, hobbies, or certain relationships in your life, or to change an attitude, habit, or pattern of behavior is never more than one choice away. As soon as you make a new choice, whatever it's about, you'll be traveling in a new direction. You might be amazed at how much power you really have.

# 24

# GET INVOLVED IN SPORTS

There is something therapeutic, satisfying, and extremely nourishing about being involved in sports. Whether it's soccer, running, or other track and field events, football, basketball, wrestling, tennis, golf, baseball, hiking, gymnastics, swimming, or whatever else you learn to enjoy, the simple act of *participating* in sports can be a life-enhancing decision. Further, it may be something you'll enjoy for the rest of your life.

Being involved in sports, at *any* level of participation—whether you're an absolute beginner, an average player, or actual champion—affects you on many levels: physical, mental, and emotional.

First, and most important, it's a physical outlet where you can do something just for the fun of it. You can let off steam, horse around, make noise (depending on the sport), and pal around with and meet new friends. It allows you to have something in common with other people. Sports give you a chance to take your mind off the rest of your life (including your problems), clear your mind, and enjoy the moment. They give you something really healthy to be enthused and passionate about, something to cheer for.

Second, sports give you a chance to improve your coordination and strength as well as your physical and mental skills. You can learn to compete, cooperate, practice good sportsmanship and teamwork, and see how well you can do. If you ask around, you'll probably find that almost everyone who is involved in sports—at any level—is really glad they are.

Further, when you are involved in sports, you always have something to do. As a teen, I loved to play tennis. I don't think I was ever bored because I could always use a little practice hitting the ball against the wall.

Finally, participating in sports—whether you win or lose—will help you stop sweating the small stuff so much. By learning to take out some of your frustrations on the field or on the court (or wherever else you play), you also can learn to be less frustrated in the rest of your life. When you expend physical energy, you release what are called endorphins in your body, which help you feel more relaxed and peaceful.

So whether it's through school, the community, or even if you have to set it up yourself, why not give sports a try? And remember, it truly doesn't matter how good you are. As long as you are participating, you are a winner!

## 25

# BECOME A TEENAGE WARRIOR

Whether we want to admit it or not, and certainly whether we like it or not, life is full of difficulties. It's an inevitable part of the package. The question becomes: Do our problems and difficulties ruin us, turn us sour and apathetic, or destroy our spirits? Or are they a source of growth, wisdom, perspective, and patience? The answer is: It completely depends on how you look at them.

Don Juan once said, "The difference between an ordinary man and a warrior is that a warrior takes everything as a challenge, while an ordinary man takes everything as a blessing or a curse." The good news is, with a slight shift in attitude, you can become a "teenage warrior," which will serve you now and for the rest of your life.

Think of the people you respect the most—people you actually know, or heroes you have great respect for. How do they respond to the challenges and difficulties in their lives? Do they whine and complain—and feel like victims? Are they resentful? Do they feel sorry for themselves and tell themselves, "I'll never get through this?" Of course not.

Now think of people, whether they are close to you—acquaintances, neighbors—or simply people you've heard of who complain about virtually everything. Those who commiserate with others, whine, stomp their feet, and fail to take responsibility for the quality of their own lives.

What's the difference between these two types of people? Is it their circumstances or the severity of the difficulties they face? No way! In fact, if you look carefully, you'll see that those people with the *most* courageous attitudes are often the ones with the biggest problems and challenges.

Some of the most remarkable teens I've ever met have had serious and/or painful physical conditions or illnesses, overcome a drug addiction, experienced poverty, or grown up without parents. And it probably wouldn't surprise you that some of the most unhappy, dissatisfied, and apathetic teens I've met come from wealthy families, have two parents who love them, are beautiful, have healthy bodies, and all the perks one could ever imagine. Indeed, circumstances don't make a person—they *reveal* her or him!

The difference between an "ordinary" teen and a "teenage warrior" lies in the way they view problems, hassles, even legitimate hardships. An ordinary teen labels things as "good" or "bad" and feels troubled by his burdens. A teenage warrior, on the other hand, tries to find a hidden gift, however small, in each hurdle she faces. I read about a Tibetan lama who was thrown into a Chinese prison for eighteen years. He said that he viewed his prison guards as his greatest teachers because they helped him to become patient and compassionate.

While that is certainly an extreme example, it does suggest that we can apply the same wisdom to the daily, less severe challenges we face. It suggests that when something goes wrong, rather than reacting as usual, feeling defeated, going crazy, or getting depressed, we can look at the situation differently. Is there something we can learn—patience, perspective, humility, generosity, perseverance, or something else? Is there some way this problem can make us better people? Do we absolutely, positively have to overreact? Or can we rise above it?

The simple act of being open to the possibility that your problems may be able to teach you something—that there just might be a hidden gift—is often enough to transform your problems into new opportunities. By keeping an open mind and looking at your problems in this way, you too can become a teenage warrior.

# 26

# PUT IT ON PAPER

It has been long recognized that there is tremendous value in putting your thoughts on paper. Whether it's a formal journal or diary, or simply random thoughts on scraps of paper, the act of writing (or typing, I suppose) is a healthy and harmless way to sort through, ponder, reflect upon, or express your feelings.

Once, when I was thirteen years old, I was furious at someone whom I discovered was talking behind my back. I was about to confront him when my mother gave me an alternate suggestion. She said, "Why don't you write a letter and really let him have it?" "Really?" I answered. "Sure," my mom said, "but don't send it. Write down exactly how you feel, then throw it away." I remember thinking "Yeah, right," but I agreed to give it a try.

The weird thing was, she was right on the mark! The simple act of writing down my feelings got them off my chest—and allowed me to let go of them. Even as I threw the letter in the trash, I felt loads better. There was no need to take the next step and actually send it; writing it was enough. The same principle applies to a diary or journal—write down your feelings and, surprisingly, you'll feel more peaceful or more complete a good percentage of the time. I'm not exactly sure why it works—it just does.

An even more powerful application of this idea is to write down your positive feelings. A popular thing to do is to keep a "gratitude journal," focusing on all that's right with your life. The reason this is so helpful is that it keeps your mind geared toward the positive aspects of life and reminds you that, although life can be difficult, there is indeed plenty to be grateful for.

In *Don't Sweat the Small Stuff . . . and It's All Small Stuff*, I made the simple suggestion to write a heartfelt letter once a week. I said that it wasn't so important to whom the letter was written—only the fact that it was written. The idea was to focus on something really positive about the person and to let him or her know of your gratitude and other feelings. You can write to someone you know—a relative, friend, teacher, or neighbor—or to someone you don't know but do admire or respect.

The response I've received from teens has been overwhelmingly positive. Teenagers from around the world have written to me telling me how helpful this idea has been. (A good number even wrote their first letter to me.) Many said it pulled them out of a funk or a bad mood; almost all said it had become a welcome and regular part of their lives that made them feel better virtually all the time. The act of putting down positive feelings on paper and sending them to someone has made a world of difference. If you think about it, give it a try. You too may be surprised at how good it can make you feel.

# 27

# DON'T EXPECT LIFE TO BE EASY OR TROUBLE-FREE

When you ask people whether they expect their life to be easy or trouble-free, almost everyone says, "Of course I don't expect that." Yet, interestingly enough, when you pay careful attention to the way people respond to minor adversity, it becomes apparent that, in reality, we often *do* expect our lives to be easy. Otherwise, we wouldn't be "sweating it" whenever life wasn't accommodating us the way we would like it to. We'd be far more accepting of the way things are rather than insisting that things be different or better.

Think about it. We expect and demand that our computer works perfectly every time, without a glitch. Why else would we go crazy and get frustrated on those rare occasions when there is a problem? Same thing with other electronic gadgets and conveniences. We're fine so long as they work as expected. If not, we're thrown off balance.

The same can be said about the expectations we often have of other people. For example, we expect others to behave in certain ways—and when they don't, we become upset. We also expect certain reactions from people—but when we don't get them, we're stressed or disappointed. Similarly, we expect things to go a certain way. We're okay as long as they go as planned. But when they don't, we lose it.

Years ago, a dear friend of mine asked me a question that, in an instant, changed the way I looked at things. I was complaining about my life and my many troubles and hassles—mostly "small stuff." He looked me in the eye and said in a sincere tone, "Richard, do you think you should be exempt from the rest of the human race?" He wasn't being condescending or mean-spirited. He simply wanted me to understand that along with the gift of life comes plenty of hassle, frustration, and difficulty. No one is exempt from this absolute inevitability. *There are no exceptions.*

I hope you'll consider this bit of wisdom as well. It's ironic, but when you remind yourself that life isn't supposed to be easy or trouble-free, in some strange way, your life begins to *seem* a bit easier and more trouble-free.

# 28

# DARE TO SHOW ENTHUSIASM

In addition to being young, teens are gifted with creativity and the willingness to be open to new ideas and new adventures. Yet without genuine enthusiasm, your inherent gifts have little chance to materialize into much.

Enthusiasm is that spark of energy and sense of interest and inspiration that ignites effort, good ideas, intention, creativity, and hard work. Enthusiastic people are imaginative, inspirational, and just plain fun to be around. I've found that while it's almost impossible to succeed without enthusiasm (regardless of how smart or gifted you might be), it's also quite difficult, with enough enthusiasm, to fail. It's that important.

Enthusiasm can get you through many difficult circumstances in your life and can help you in all you do. In high school and later in college, my enthusiasm made up for the lack of ease I had in my subjects. For the most part, my instructors sensed my enthusiasm and did everything they could to help me—my enthusiasm was contagious, so they wanted me to succeed. In my career, the connection between enthusiasm and success has been even more obvious. It has helped me to make my dream of spreading positive, life-enhancing messages to others come true. Virtually everyone I've come into contact with—my publisher, producers at talk shows, groups I speak to, the general public—has told me that one of the things they admire most about me is my enthusiasm. Almost never is it my intellect, work ethic, business savvy, or something else. It's not that these things aren't important, it's just that those aren't the things that people feel from you. What people feel is your sincerity and your enthusiasm.

Think of all the successful people you admire. Whether it's a sports star, a teen idol or other entertainer, a teacher, parent, businessperson, author, or Internet wizard—the top people, those who shine, have one thing in common: enthusiasm for what they are doing.

I've hired a number of people to work for me and know many others who have done the same. From my perspective, enthusiasm weighs more heavily than almost any other factor in my decision to hire or not hire someone for a job. In other words, while grades, intellect, and other factors might be important, no one (certainly not I) really wants to work with someone who is a "downer" to be around, someone who sulks, frowns, lacks positive energy, or appears to be indifferent. Very simply, others don't want to have much to do with people who are apathetic or lack enthusiasm.

Even if you're in the habit of being a little negative, pessimistic, or indifferent—and even if your friends are that way too—I encourage you to dare to be enthusiastic! Smile at adults. Express genuine interest and enthusiasm in all you do, and be inquisitive about what others are doing. This slight attitude adjustment, as long as it's sincere, may be just what you need to jump-start the life of your dreams.

## 29

# FIND PEACE THROUGH GIVING

There is nothing quite like the feeling of knowing that you've done something really nice for someone else, whether the person acknowledges it or, for that matter, even knows that you've done it. If you think of those things that feel the best to you, I'll bet you'll agree that giving to others is at or near the top of your list.

One of my personal role models, or heroes, is Mother Teresa, a spiritual leader who was known during her lifetime as a teacher of peace, goodwill, charity, kindness, and love. My favorite quote of hers was, "We cannot do great things on this Earth. We can only do small things with great love." What she meant was that we don't have to change the world with our actions; we only make a small, ongoing contribution. When asked the question, "What can someone do to become happier?" she and many other spiritual people have said, "Do something nice for someone else." You'll find that when you're nice, the world will seem good. When you're kind and thoughtful, the world will return the favor to you.

The small things you do can be practically anything—an act of kindness or sharing, for example. One day, my youngest daughter had forgotten to take her lunch to school. A classmate of hers, whom she barely even knew, offered to share her meal with her. That simple gesture meant so much to my daughter that she glowed with joy all day with the realization that "someone would be so nice."

I was very impressed by a group of teens I met in Alabama. I asked them to share with me some of the ways they had expressed their giving. Several responded by saying that it was fun and easy, as well as tremendously rewarding, to help someone with homework, or a jump-shot, or by teaching something, or helping a person out of a jam—all great ideas. One student was working on a brilliant idea. She was trying to set up a class project where everyone in the class would donate one dollar, and together, as a class, they would sponsor a needy child overseas. Can you imagine what would happen if every school had great ideas like this one? The whole world would be kinder and would have to endure less suffering.

Sometimes, sticking up for the underdog or refusing to pick on someone who is being taunted by others is a small act of love, something you'll feel good about. Then again, at times saying hello or simply smiling at someone can be enough. You also can be giving by helping someone who is lost to find his way—or by helping someone new to your school to feel more welcome, or remembering to write thank-you notes, or any of thousands of other little things.

The point is, whenever you give to others, and however you choose to do it, you'll notice that your stress will be reduced and you'll feel better about yourself and the world—guaranteed. There's no question that one of the most important secrets in the world is that by becoming more giving, you'll become happier as well. So, spend some time thinking about ways you can be even more giving to others. I can assure you, it will be well worth it.

# 30

# BECOME 25 PERCENT
# LESS CRITICAL

This is a helpful strategy for two reasons. First, virtually anyone can become 25 percent less critical if he sets his mind to it. And second, with each lessening of criticism, you'll experience a corresponding increase in your own level of satisfaction. You'll also find yourself being more open-minded, and your learning curve will sharpen. You'll be more fun to be around too.

As you embark on this strategy, be prepared to be a little shocked. You're likely to discover that you and your friends expend a huge amount of energy on criticism. Most of us find ways to be critical of practically everything. We're critical of the world, politics, people who see things differently from the way we do, those who look different, act different, and so forth. We're often critical of our family members, our school and teachers, people who do well in life as well as those who struggle.

The way to go about becoming less critical is very straightforward. You simply begin paying attention to what you think and talk about, particularly when you are being critical. As I said, at first it's a real eye-opener. Thirteen-year-old John may have said it best: "It was weird. I found myself being critical of other people who were being critical." I have to admit that I've done this too.

That's pretty much all you have to do; the rest will take care of itself.

You may start saying things to yourself like, "Wow, I'm critical a lot of the time—maybe I could be less so," or something like that. You'll begin catching yourself when you're being too critical—and dropping the criticism. You can even think of it as a game you play with yourself. When your mind drifts toward inappropriate, unnecessary, or unfair criticism, you simply dismiss it before it has a chance to develop.

This has nothing to do with letting go of appropriate criticism, because certainly there are many times when it's important or appropriate to be critical. However, I'm referring to the habitual, mean-spirited, or simply knee-jerk types of criticism that usually stem from gossip, or habit, or simply from a dose of too much negativity.

A vast majority of teens whom I've asked to try this have said that, since being less critical, they like themselves much more than before. My guess is that you'll find this strategy eye-opening. But whatever you do, don't be too hard on yourself. What's the sense of being critical about your own tendency to be critical? Keep in mind that you're doing something about it.

# 31

# WALK AWAY

It would be difficult to estimate just how much stress I have avoided, minimized, and prevented by my willingness to walk away from conflict. I can assure you, however, that it's been an enormous factor that has contributed greatly to my own happiness and peace of mind.

Many people think it's weak to walk away. I disagree. Anyone can fight, argue, bicker, or battle. That's easy, and most people do it. It takes a strong and, I believe, wise person, however, to be willing to walk away.

I'm not only talking about walking away from physical confrontations, although that's part of it. I'm talking about being able to walk away from arguments and conflicts that are likely to lead to stress, heartache, agony, anxiety, or hassle.

I'm lucky that a vast majority of the people I work with, spend time with, or partner with in some capacity are ethical, wonderful people. From time to time, however, I run across people who are unreasonable, argumentative, adversarial, defensive, conflict-oriented, or just plain difficult. Some people seem to try to "pick a fight," almost like sport. I'm sure you've met some of them.

There are people who love to threaten and hassle others, some who actually enjoy lawsuits and other types of conflict. I was recently threatened with a suit by someone simply because I had agreed to help someone else—and this person didn't like it! It was one of the most ridiculous, frivolous things I had ever seen. And while many people I discussed it with were urging me to fight back—sue him for harassment, or whatever—I chose to walk away. Why? Was I weak? I don't think so.

Think about what happens when you engage yourself in this type of conflict (or something similar). Think of all the energy you spend, and the hours and hours you spend thinking about it. You end up angry, frustrated, and stressed. You create hatred and resentment. You spend your valuable time discussing it with others. Your head is filled with negativity. You try to prove your position. You argue and try to make the other party wrong. You hire lawyers. You go to court. And to what end? You get to feel like you are "right."

In my personal example, as is almost always the case, the situation faded, the urgency diminished and eventually resolved itself. Had I chosen to fight back and escalate the conflict, something as stupid as this could have become much bigger. Far better, I believe, to not sweat the small stuff.

Robert, a sixteen-year-old, was encouraged by his buddies to punch someone who was, allegedly, going to report something he had done to the principal of their school. They urged him on, saying "You can't let him get away with that." He did punch the guy. He then kicked him when he was down and seriously hurt him. While his buddies, the enthusiasts, walked away scot-free, Robert was arrested and sentenced to a year in juvenile hall. Had he simply walked away, a year of misery could have been avoided.

The same principle applies to so many situations—someone argues with you, cuts you off on the freeway, accuses you of something, corrects you in front of a friend, or has a need to be "right." You might have a disagreement with someone who can't "agree to disagree" and has a need to battle over it. The specific situations are endless. All of us are involved, from time to time, in circumstances where we have a choice of battling to prove that we are "right" or simply walking away.

While there are certainly times when it's either wise or necessary to fight back, it's not as often as you might think. Most of the time, it's wiser and more practical to simply walk away. Doing so will save you more grief, hassle, and aggravation than you can possibly imagine.

# 32

# ALLOW A NEW IDEA
# TO COME TO YOU

Have you ever noticed how tempting it is, when you're uncertain about something, to struggle with or get "stuck" in your thinking and to try even harder? Or to force your thoughts or think too hard? If so, you're not alone. It's a universal problem.

I like this strategy because it's one where the idea is to try less, not more! In fact, the less effort, the better.

All of us have within ourselves a great deal of wisdom, something you might call innate mental health. Unfortunately, however, this inner wisdom is often interfered with by all the confusing and conflicting thoughts, ideas, plans, and fears that fill our minds. Yet just as the sun is still up in the sky even when all you see are clouds, your wisdom is in there somewhere, waiting for you to call on it.

Wisdom is best called upon for issues pertaining to the heart—for example, when you need to know how to mend a relationship, get along better with your parents or siblings, help a friend who is struggling, move forward after making a mistake, make a difficult decision—or when you can't figure out what to do next. These types of issues, and others like them, require not a brilliant intellect but a sense of softness, a clear mind, and plenty of wisdom.

The next time you need help with a matter of the heart, try something a little different. Rather than sorting through the pros and cons, filling your mind with facts, and going back and forth with your thinking, over and over again, allow your thoughts to settle. You might imagine your mind to be one of those toys filled with water and fake snowflakes. When you shake it up, there is snow everywhere and plenty of confusion, but when you allow it to be still, the snow settles calmly to the ground. In a similar way, you can relax your mind, let your thoughts go, and allow them to be calm. Then, with a clear mind, tell yourself that you need a wise and appropriate answer to your problem, issue, or dilemma. Then, again, clear your mind and let go of your thoughts. For a few minutes, don't even concern yourself with the outcome.

What sometimes happens is quite fascinating. Instead of your having to actively pursue your best ideas by trying to come up with them, instead, new ideas will begin to come to you, as if from out of the blue. Rather than actively thinking, forcing, or struggling, you are simply allowing the ideas to percolate and surface on their own. The entire process may take only a few minutes, sometimes a bit longer. Other times nothing will come to you right away, but later, when you least expect it, an answer will pop into your mind.

The reason this works so well is that you've already stored the facts in your mind. The answer is in there somewhere. All you're doing now is allowing the answer a chance to surface!

A couple I knew many years ago had a seventeen-year-old daughter who was having a hard time. She was so caught up in the dramas of daily living, the confusion of not knowing what to do after high school, and the fear of leaving her friends that she had become unable to make virtually any decisions regarding her future. Her parents, instructors, counselor—even her friends—had all encouraged her to "think it through," "figure it out," and so forth. The problem was, the more she thought about it, the more confused and frightened she became.

After hearing about this simple idea and experimenting with it themselves, her parents gently suggested she give this a try. All they said was, "Forget about making decisions for a while. Something will come to you when you least expect it."

To make a long story short, they were right. With the benefit of a clear mind, their daughter knew, within a few days, that what she really wanted to do was attend a local community college. What was most interesting to her parents was both the certainty of her decision and the fact that she hadn't even been actively considering attending college. She had discussed the possibility of modeling, acting school, and getting a job, but hadn't considered or discussed college for more than a year. Yet, with a relaxed mind, her answer was easy and clear.

Some of your answers may be dramatic or surprising; others, very simple and ordinary. However, one thing is certain. If "figuring something out" is going to work, it usually does so pretty quickly. If that's not working, you might want to experiment with this strategy; it may help you sort things out.

## 33

# GET READY EARLY

I'm thrilled at the number of people who have told me how much this suggestion has helped them. I'm confident that, once you see the logic behind it, it will seem as obvious to you as the need to eat or sleep! The problem is, before you convince yourself of the importance of getting ready early, you'll see dozens of really good reasons why you "can't."

We live in busy times. Most of us feel that we're too busy and stretched for time. When you ask teens and adults alike what their perceived sources of stress is, many will say, "Not enough time," or, "I'm always in a hurry."

Usually there are certain times of the day that are even crazier than the rest. In our family, for example, it's the early morning. Although there are only four of us, it seems there are a hundred things to take care of and prepare for each and every day. If we're rushed, it's extremely stressful. If we're not, it's a nonissue.

It's fascinating to see how the same number of activities is experienced very differently, depending on how much time we allow. I'm convinced that one of the reasons people feel in such an enormous hurry is that they fail to give themselves adequate time to get ready. For example, if it takes an hour to do everything they need to do, most people will give themselves a *maximum* of one hour in which to do it. Never more, often far less. So, if everything goes smoothly and there are no unexpected problems, hassles, phone calls, lost items, or other time-consuming constraints, they will just make it if they hurry. The entire day is set up to be stressful, even if everything goes smoothly.

The nature of being in a hurry is stressful. You're rushing around, wondering if you'll make it and thinking about how busy you are. You might be thinking about what consequences there will be if you're late, or who might be mad at you. This type of thinking is stressful. It's also when you're hurried that you're most likely to misplace things, make mistakes, or forget something when you walk out the door. This too causes stress.

It's interesting, however, to listen to the excuses of people when they are late. "I didn't have enough time" is the number-one excuse. Number two is "I had too much to do." Seldom do you hear the truth, which is "I didn't give myself enough time." See the difference? In one instance you see yourself as a victim of time. You'll probably continue to do the same thing often because you see the problem as being out of your control. In the other instance, however, you see yourself as empowered, as having the capacity to give yourself additional time.

Sometimes we do allow ourselves enough time, but instead of getting all the way, 100 percent ready, we get what I like to call "almost ready." Then, at the last minute, we scramble to do those remaining few things—make a lunch, find our books, shave, gather our stuff, search for our shoes, make that urgent phone call, or whatever. We scramble and we feel pressured. This feeling of pressure can affect our entire day, encouraging us to feel uptight and to sweat the small stuff.

Most of this time stress can be eliminated from your life forever. All it takes is your willingness to see that the problem is self-created. As hard as it is to admit, it's usually not a lack of time that is the problem— instead, the problem is not giving yourself quite enough time. It's not getting *all* the way ready early enough.

If you usually give yourself an hour, for example, to get ready to go somewhere, experiment with 50 percent more time, or in this example, an extra thirty minutes. (You can adjust as needed.) Notice the difference in the quality of your experience—the lack of feeling pressured and stressed. Notice how the identical routine, with the same number of things to do, feels less stressful. And be sure, while you're at it, to get *all* the way ready (rather than almost ready) well before it's time to go. It's strange, but often as little as five or ten minutes can be the difference between a stressful day in which you're constantly "catching up" and a peaceful day in which you have plenty of time.

You can apply the same logic to longer-term projects as well. There is something quite peaceful about doing a book report, for example, well before the actual due date instead of cramming the night before. Or sending a birthday card a week early instead of hoping it will arrive on time. The number of actual applications for this strategy are vast. However you choose to use it, I hope it helps you as much as it has helped me.

## 34

# AVOID THE 90–10 TRAP

To me, this is one of the strangest habits that people get into. What's more, it seems to afflict almost everybody. Once you see how crazy and illogical it is, however, I'm hoping that you too will see it as a trap.

The "90–10 trap" stems from an observation I've made (that has been verified by hundreds of people) that most of us tend to focus our attention, thinking, and conversations on the worst 10 percent of our lives. The 90 stands for 90 percent of what happens during our day, which is usually pretty good, and the 10 stands for the remaining 10 percent, which is usually problematic and filled with hassle.

I call it a trap because most people seem to focus on what's wrong with life instead of what is, generally, okay. Obviously, every day is different and some days really are bad. But the way it typically plays out is this: Suppose, for illustration's sake, that you had ten things to do during the day. Nine of them go reasonably well. The other one doesn't. Which one do you think about the most that evening? Which one do you discuss with your parents, siblings, or friends? You get the idea.

Suppose, in addition, that you interact with ten people that day. Nine of them were pleasant and respectful, but the other one was a real jerk! Rarely, when I've asked people about their day, has someone said,

"You know, it was a pretty good day. Almost everyone was nice to me and friendly." Instead, a more typical answer might be, "There was this real jerk, and let me tell you what he did."

Let me assure you that I'm not making a case for not sharing the dramatic parts of your day, or the hassles or problems. I'm also not suggesting that it's always necessary to focus on what's good and right with your life. That's going way too far. I'm talking about creating a little more balance in what you choose to focus on. I'm suggesting that the 90 percent (or 80 or 70 or whatever the percentage happens to be) is also worthy of at least some of your attention.

It would be like looking at a beautiful painting and, instead of appreciating the beauty, focusing on the fact that you don't like the artist's signature. Again, I'm not saying you have to like the signature, but it might be a good idea to ask yourself why it is that you automatically focus on the one part you don't like. If you focus more on what you like, you'll enjoy the painting far more than if you zero in on the poor signature. Likewise, you'll enjoy your life more and have a better experience if you focus a greater percentage of your attention on the parts that go well instead of zeroing in on the problems and hassles.

The idea here is to simply become aware of the tendency and to notice when you're focusing too much on the negative. What sometimes happens when you apply this strategy is that you'll begin to realize that, while there are certainly aspects to life that are hard and stressful, there are also many things to be grateful for. And when you notice those things—and think about them and talk about them—your life will seem better and a bit less stressful. It's easier to deal with the stress and hassles of life when you're also aware of what's right with your life.

Just for fun, the next time you talk to your parents or a friend, ask them to tell you about the best part of their day. Ask them if they had any good experiences or whether anyone was exceptionally kind, funny, or whatever. Ask them if they had a nice lunch or if they had any interesting ideas. You'll probably catch them off guard! On the other hand, you'll be helping them to experience the other part of life—the good part.

# 35

# BE THE ROLE MODEL

There's a lot of talk about the importance of having role models, and there's no question that it is important. It's equally important, however, to *be* a good role model. Rather than leaving it up to famous people who often fall far short, *you* can become the person others look up to.

When you think of a role model, what do you envision? I think of someone who sets a great example to others in the areas that most of us consider to be important—kindness, ethics, generosity, caring, patience, thoughtfulness, dedication, and hard work. But if you think about it, you don't have to be famous to be these things. *Anyone* can be a role model if he decides that it's important. Being a world-class athlete, entertainer, politician, or anything else like that has nothing to do with it. These people can be role models too, but they do not have a corner on the market!

My two children have a handful of great teens they look up to as role models. These role models are, to me (and to my kids), far more important than some famous politician pretending to have "family values" or some famous athlete, even if he or she is doing great work for the community. The teens my kids look up to have normal teenage lives, yet they are kind to everyone, especially kids; they try hard in school; work hard at their jobs; and try to be really great human beings. To me, that's a great role model!

There is something very special about knowing that you are trying hard to be a good role model, that you are someone who cares about others. Imagine how good it would feel to know that, when people think about you or talk about you, they describe you as "a really nice person," or "someone who would never hurt anyone," or "always ethical."

Achievements and accomplishments are important, and I would never suggest otherwise. On the other hand, they can take you only so far. In the end, what really matters—and what people remember you for, and how you value yourself—is all about the type of person you are and the type of role model you become. How do you treat people? How do you handle stressful situations? Are you fair, kind, considerate, helpful, willing to be of service, hardworking, etc.?

I would suggest that if you are these things, then you already are a role model. Whether you're well known or popular is irrelevant. You're affecting people by your very presence, by the way you act, the decisions you make, and the way you are with others. When you know this about yourself, it's easy to feel good about who you are. And when you feel good about who you are, your life will be relatively stress-free. More important, you'll be happy.

## 36

# DON'T UNDERESTIMATE
# YOURSELF

Many of us inadvertently create stress in our lives by making the mistake of underestimating ourselves. Failing to have adequate confidence in our abilities, intuition, and wisdom means we must rely on others to guide and direct us.

The reason this is so potentially stressful is that it encourages us to seek acknowledgment, acceptance, and approval from outside sources—peers, parents, friends, and others—rather than from within ourselves. If we don't get the approval we're looking for, we feel anxious and stressed. And even if we do get it, we're always wondering if it will last. Either way is stressful and filled with pressure. It's when you feel pressure that you're most likely to sweat the small stuff, make mistakes, and become unhappy.

On the other hand, when you give yourself the credit you deserve and when you have confidence in yourself, you are in charge and have control over the acknowledgment you are seeking. You can learn to be proud of yourself, knowing you've done your best, regardless of what anyone else thinks. When this happens, your confidence will soar because you'll be less distracted and will spend far less energy concerning yourself with what other people say or think about you.

Everyone I know who has an adequate supply of self-confidence has it because, at some point in her life, she decided she needed it. These people have realized that, no matter how hard they try or how successful they become, there will always be people who find fault with and criticize them. There will always be people who still think they aren't good enough. Furthermore, they come to the realization that if they don't feel good about themselves and their efforts, it makes no difference how much praise or recognition they receive—or how well they do in life—because they won't feel it. Those with genuine self-confidence make a conscious decision that, although guidance is always welcome and approval and acknowledgment are always nice, ultimately the only lasting confidence comes from within. It's as if they realize that no one is going to be able to hand them self-confidence. Rather, it's a decision that must be made.

Confidence doesn't only come with success. It works in reverse as well. In other words, it's true that getting a good grade helps create confidence in your abilities as a student—that's positive reinforcement. It's also true, however, that knowing you are a bright, intelligent, talented, and wise person, and admitting this to yourself on a regular basis, helps you get the good grade to begin with. Confidence creates the inner atmosphere to succeed.

Even if you are a straight-A student, a champion athlete, gifted in music or drama, or have a unique talent, your self-confidence still will have to come from you. You still will have to decide that you have self-worth and that you are worthy of self-confidence. This shouldn't be difficult because it's true.

I once had a conversation with a junior high school student who was about to embark on a complicated research project. I remember asking her, "Do you know how you're going to go about it?" Her answer speaks to the point of this strategy. She said, "Not really, but I'm certain I'll be able to do it." Despite the lack of an immediate solution, there was strength in her answer. She had confidence she could pull it off, regardless of how much work was involved. This type of confidence comes from reminding yourself, over and over again, that you are a competent, bright person who will find a way to rise to the occasion, whatever the occasion happens to be. Believe in yourself—you're worth it!

# 37

# GET OVER
# COMPLETION ANXIETY

To be honest, I don't know if there really is something called completion anxiety or if it's something I made up. I do know, however, that a huge number or people are afflicted with it! I also know that it creates an enormous amount of stress for those who have it.

I define completion anxiety as the tendency to "not quite" finish something, presumably because it makes you anxious or uncomfortable in some way. There's a way that we "almost" finish things, but not all the way—homework, dishes, discussing uncomfortable issues, chores, or work, for example.

If you have ever hired a carpenter or handyman (or woman) to do some work around the home, have you noticed how even very talented and hardworking people have a tendency to finish almost everything but leave a little part of it undone? Have you either experienced this yourself, or have friends who are in the habit of finishing all but part of an assignment? If you're asked to do the dishes or clean your room, have you seen how hard it is to bite the bullet and do it all?

Who knows why so many of us have this tendency? Perhaps it's because we feel that if we finish all the way, we'll be asked to do even more—or that if we finish, there will be nothing left. Maybe we resent being asked to begin with. Maybe it's something else.

But if your goal is to have less stress in your life, take a look at the implications. First, think about the stress of always having things hang over your head. When something isn't done, it's hard to put it behind you, check it off your list, and forget about it. It's always looming and tugging on your attention. It's a burden.

In addition, it's a pain to have people—parents, teachers, employers, clients—breathing down your neck and applying pressure to you. It's hard to have people disappointed in you, asking, reminding, or nagging you to finish.

The problem is, most people have a tendency to notice what we haven't done instead of what we have done. Right or wrong, parents will often notice the 10 percent of the room that isn't clean instead of the 90 percent that is. Or a teacher will ask, "Why didn't you do this one?" rather than saying, "I think it's great you did most of them." If I turned this book in with ninety-nine strategies done, but not all one hundred, my publisher would be more concerned with the missing strategy than the ninety-nine that were done well.

Recently I hired someone to fix something at my home. The person did an excellent job, technically, but left a sloppy mess on our floor. To be honest, I was more concerned with the mess than I was impressed with his work. I took it as a given that the job would be done well—but that was overshadowed by the thirty minutes it took to clean up the man's mess. Whether he cares or not is a different issue, but he won't be hired again by us, nor will he receive any referrals. Had he taken a few extra minutes to complete the job, it would have been a nonissue.

One of the simplest ways to reduce this type of stress is to make an effort to finish things—all the way, 100 percent—whenever it's within your power to do so. You'll eliminate tons of stress because you won't have to think about it anymore, and you won't have anyone bugging you about it. People won't have any ammunition against you.

The way I look at it is this. You probably intend to finish it at some point anyway, just not now. But if you do it now, rather than later, you won't have to be stressed and hassled in the meantime. Whether it's something specific, such as a task or chore, or an entire list of things that's looming heavily on your mind, the extra effort to complete things, whenever possible, pays big dividends in the quality of your life.

# 38

# SEE THE POSSIBILITIES

One of the secrets to staying calm and happy is to remain hopeful. And, without question, one of the best ways to remain hopeful is to see the possibilities.

It's easy, of course, to lose hope and to be unable to see the possibilities. This happens whenever we get overly absorbed in the difficulties that we are facing and lose our perspective, when our optimism is overshadowed by fear. We forget how many times we've overcome obstacles in the past and just how resilient we really are.

The best way that I know of to see the possibilities—whether it's the possibility of meeting a challenge, winning, achieving a goal, or overcoming a problem—is to think back on your life and remember how many times you've done it before. Think back to all the times you felt certain you wouldn't be able to do something, yet, in the end, you succeeded. Remember how convinced you were that you'd never be able to figure out a math procedure, or meet any new friends, or survive your parents' latest fight, or a consequence levied on you. Think about all the times you convinced yourself, "This challenge is different—I'll never get through this one."

Yet here you are. You've made it through every single challenge you've faced—and each one of them helped you become the person you are today. It's pretty awesome when you think about it. And when you look at it like this, it's illogical to think you can't do it again—because you can!

Beth, a sixteen-year-old, had moved three times in three years. Just about the time she made some new friends, her dad would be transferred again and that would be that! With barely any notice, she would be in a new town, at a new school, not knowing a single person.

It would have been really easy for her to give up and feel sorry for herself. Instead, she decided to stay focused on the possibilities and to always keep in mind that she had been able to meet new friends before.

She told me that this simple decision was the very thing that saved her. Rather than burying herself in her own misery and sadness, Beth kept her hope alive for meeting new friends. And guess what? She did. Each time she moved, her eyes and heart were open to meeting new people and her optimism led the way to new friends. Here's the best part. When she looked back on those last three years, she wouldn't have changed a thing. There wasn't a single friend she would have missed along the way; her moves were worth it, the pain and all.

When you focus on possibilities instead of limitations, a whole new world will open up to you, a world of optimism and new opportunity. Because you will be less distracted by your worries and fear, it will be much easier to get through things, no matter how difficult. And, because your spirit will be filled with optimism, you'll be happier each and every day.

# 39

# PRACTICE NOT SWEATING
# THE *REALLY* SMALL STUFF

We live in a very stressful world. Therefore, probably there are many reasons why we're seeing so many drastic acts of violence and examples of unhappiness and frustration involving teens. I won't pretend to have all the answers. I suspect, however, that a contributing factor to the problems we're seeing is that very few of us learn, at an early enough age, to not sweat the small stuff. If you think about it, there are some pretty important implications stemming from this.

What do you suppose would happen, for example, to someone who never learned to let things go? What if every single little thing, every small hassle, and every little nuisance was blown way out of proportion and treated like a giant emergency? What if your role models taught you to freak out over the slightest glitch in your plans or the tiniest mistake made? Logically, if you can't handle even the smallest things with some degree of patience, perspective, and the ability to keep your cool, then, as the stakes get bigger, so will your reactions. In other words, someone who can't handle a situation like a little static on the television screen— or a misplaced toy—certainly isn't going to be able to handle bigger things later on, like being dropped by a girlfriend or boyfriend, criticism by peers, or getting a poor grade on an important test.

And while few of us freak out to this degree over every small thing, most of us do, to one degree or another, lack the necessary perspective, patience, and "cool" required to live a happy life with a minimal amount of stress.

To get this perspective, the trick seems to be to start with the really small stuff and build on your success. To begin with, you can choose anything that you think of as slightly irritating yet small and relatively insignificant. You might, for example, try to practice being more patient with a sibling who walks into your room without knocking. Or, despite the temptation, stop talking to your friends about a weird quirk that one of your teachers has. Or maybe your mom makes you do something around the house that you don't like to do, but is nevertheless necessary. Perhaps you could practice doing it without feeling or acting annoyed. Practicing something like these things or something entirely different is okay. What you're trying to do is to have experiences where you are intentionally and consciously responding with less reactivity and less harshly to things you are used to getting uptight about. You're practicing not sweating the small stuff.

What happens, if you practice this with different situations for a while, is that you'll start to accept the fact that there will always be things about day-to-day living that are either less than ideal or slightly irritating. But you'll begin to expend less negative energy on these things, and that will result in a less stressful life. You'll have more energy for enjoyment, friendships, and achievements. Pretty soon, the things that used to bother you won't bother you at all. In fact, you'll start to put more and more situations into the category of "It's not worth sweating over."

Life's little irritations will always be a drag to deal with until you learn to see them as less significant. Once you do, however, your stress will go down, your performance will be enhanced, and your life will be more fun again.

# 40

# DON'T KEEP YOUR PAIN A SECRET

It's hard enough being in emotional pain, but it's important not to compound the pain by keeping it all to yourself. When you are in pain, don't keep it a secret. Instead, use this time to reach out to others. Doing so will make you feel empowered and will help you heal more quickly and completely. Being with other people while you are suffering is often very comforting and nourishing. People are an important source of support and strength.

Some people keep their pain to themselves because they feel that they are being a burden to friends or family members. That's usually not the case. Think of how readily available you would be if a good friend, a parent, or a sibling came to you in pain. I'll bet you'd drop everything to lend a loving ear.

Over the years I've known many therapists. I've often asked them what they felt was their greatest contribution to their clients or patients. Many have suggested that perhaps the most important gift they shared with someone is simply a genuine, caring, listening ear. There is something special and healing about being listened to while you are in pain. Unquestionably it helps release an inner healing process that exists within each of us.

Obviously, not everyone can afford to see a therapist. But if seeing a professional is an option, it's worth looking into. Many schools have a counselor that may be available to help, as do many churches and places of worship. Then there are always your friends and family—who, quite possibly, might be the best listeners of all. They know you best and care about you the most.

Although many teens think of themselves as too shy to try it, a regular massage can be extremely healing. Appropriate physical touch is incredibly important, particularly since many teens are rarely touched. Studies show that people need to be touched, and a good back rub is one of the most wonderful things you can ever experience.

Like therapy, a professional massage can be expensive, so not everyone will be able to get one. However, perhaps someone in your family, or a friend, would like to trade back rubs with you. I'll bet someone would jump at the chance. My daughter Kenna and I trade back rubs all the time, and, quite frankly, it's one of our favorite things to do together. To be honest, I've met only a small number of people in my entire lifetime—teens and everyone else—who didn't love a good back rub.

I know that being in emotional pain isn't "small stuff." Yet I felt it was important to include this strategy because many teens turn inward when they are in pain rather than baring their soul to someone else. It's always nice to have people to talk to. It's especially important if you are in pain.

# 41

# MAKE A GOOD FIRST IMPRESSION

If you keep this particular strategy in mind, it will prevent a great deal of stress from occurring in your life. By making a good first impression, you won't have to "undo" or reverse any negative first impressions someone has about you.

Like it or not, first impressions are very important. I've heard it said that people form their initial opinions of us in the first minute of contact. The reason it's important to get off to a good start is that, once an opinion is formed, it's difficult to alter. So, if people see you as unfriendly, disrespectful, or lacking good manners (even if you didn't intend to come across that way), they will be unlikely to go out of their way to be nice or helpful to you, should that become necessary or desired. They might avoid you, talk behind your back, or share their negative feelings with others. In some instances, they might be downright mean or unfriendly to you. You've given them no reason to act otherwise. It's those negative first impressions that contribute to the phrase, "I don't know what it is about that person, but I don't like him."

On the other hand, if someone likes you right off the bat—if you make a good first impression—he or she is likely, at worst, to be neutral where you are concerned. In many instances, the person will go out of his way to be nice to you. That's a highly leveraged way to make your life easier. In other words, a tiny bit of effort now equals a great deal of benefit from that point on.

When you get off to a good start, your positive impression tends to feed on itself. You're nice, so the people you meet like you right away. They have a good feeling about you and think of you in positive terms. When they talk to you, your discussions will be about positive things. When they talk to others, and your name comes up, you'll be discussed in a positive light. If you ever have questions, or a need a favor, those people have no reason whatsoever to avoid helping you or answering your questions.

One of the worst first impressions I ever made was when I was a teenager and was introduced to a neighbor. At the time I was being introduced, I was with a friend. The two of us were aloof and, in retrospect, a bit disrespectful. We weren't horrible, but we were far from gracious. I made no eye contact and instead of saying, "It's nice to meet you, sir," I mumbled something under my breath.

Looking back, my failed first impression caused me a great deal of unnecessary hassle. That neighbor didn't want much to do with me. He wouldn't allow me into his yard, he complained about my dog a great deal, and he always seemed to be bothered by something I was doing. I'm relatively certain that, had I simply taken thirty seconds to be pleasant, respectful, and friendly, our relationship would have taken a different direction.

When you make a good first impression, not only are you doing the right thing by being gracious and sincere, but you are doing yourself an enormous favor as well. The tiniest amount of effort in this area will make your life easier and less stressful for the rest of your life.

## 42

# BE CAREFUL TO AVOID
# THE "I'LL SHOW YOU" TRAP

A friend shared with me a story about a teen named Sean who was angry with his parents. He wanted to teach them a lesson or get back at them in some way. He thought the best way to do it would be to fail his math class. He felt this would "show them" because both of his parents were high school math teachers.

The problem was, he actually liked math and was really good at it.

My friend offered the following solution. She asked him, "Is it possible to go ahead and try hard in the class and then convince your school to give you two report cards—one with your real grade and one with an F? That way, you get it both ways—a good grade for yourself and a failed grade for your parents."

Sean laughed so hard and thought it was such a great idea that he got the point.

The point, of course, is that all of us get frustrated. When we do, it's tempting to become vindictive and fall into the "I'll show you" trap. The problem is, it really is a trap because it's self-destructive. It's true that Sean would have shocked and disappointed his parents. Yet he, not his parents, was the one who ultimately would have had to pay the price. He would have created tons of catch-up work for himself and greatly reduced his long-term options for his life after high school.

All of us have made this mistake, but that doesn't mean it's a good idea. I knew a young woman in high school who loved to sing. She wouldn't be in the choir, however, because she was determined to "show her parents." I'd bet any amount of money that today, looking back, she wishes she hadn't been so stubborn.

I know it's tough when you're mad—it is for me too. It's tempting to lash out and prove a point. Yet if you can take a step back and avoid this trap, you may be able to prevent your own goals and passions from being destroyed or adversely affected. You'll actually get a ton of satisfaction in knowing that you're too strong to fall for this one. You'll get the last laugh after all.

# 43

# EXPERIENCE PERFECT

# IMPERFECTION

A huge, sometimes overwhelming source of stress for teens is the perceived need for perfection. Whether with regard to oneself—one's weight, hair, looks, a poor test score, or failed effort—or related to someone else—the way someone acts, looks, or chooses to live—or just life in general, perfectionism is inconsistent with happiness. If you think about it, the need for perfection and the desire for inner peace are in conflict with each other.

Whenever we need something to be "perfect," or better than it is, we are, by definition, dissatisfied. Rather than being grateful or satisfied for what we have and therefore happy, instead we are fixated on what's wrong, what's missing or lacking, what needs improvement, and what must be different.

Over and over I've heard teens say, "But if I want to be my best, I can't be satisfied with who I am or how I'm doing." That single attitude, left in place, pretty much guarantees a life of frustration. How can you be happy if you decide, in advance, that you're never going to be satisfied with yourself?

This strategy has nothing at all to do with not doing your absolute best, striving hard toward your goals, or ceasing to be competitive. Instead, it has to do with being less focused on shortcomings, failures, and deficiencies. It has to do with catching yourself when you fall into the trap of insisting that things be better—or that you look better, or do better, or that others act differently—before you allow yourself to be happy.

As a teen, Jane learned never to be satisfied. So when her goal of getting into a certain college didn't happen, she spent the next four years at the school she was admitted to, dissatisfied. Rather than enjoy her college experience, she spent four years living in regret and sadness, disappointed in herself that she wasn't "better."

I call this strategy "experience perfect imperfection" because as you let go of the need to be perfect, you begin to have the experience that there is actually perfection *within* the imperfection. Despite the way it sometimes appears on the surface, God knows what He is doing, the Universe knows what it is doing, everything is "perfect" in its own way.

In other words, you begin to realize that we are exactly where we need to be, even if we can't see it at the time. The mistakes we make are part of our journey, even though we don't like to make them and certainly do our best to avoid them.

Looking back on her life, Jane realized that the college she went to was, in fact, "perfect" for her. She went on to have a brilliant career. She met her husband-to-be. They had a family, and she has learned to be happy. The way she learned to be happy was to see that just because something doesn't appear perfect doesn't mean that it isn't. She had the experience of perfect imperfection.

You can too! As you let go of the need for everything to be perfect, you'll realize that in most instances, it already is—in its own way.

# 44

# DARE TO BE ETHICAL

Most people acknowledge that being ethical is the right thing to do. Being ethical means being fair and reasonable and not being greedy. It means you're interested in not only what's best for you, but what's honest and what's right.

There's another aspect to being ethical, however, that is worth knowing about. It's the part that takes your stress away. Something almost magical happens to your spirits when you know in your heart that you are an honest, ethical person no matter what.

We hired fourteen-year-old Alice to do some baby-sitting. One night we got home fairly late by our usual standards. I drove Alice home and handed her what I thought was the money I owed her for her six hours of work. She thanked me and went inside.

When I got home ten minutes later, the phone rang and it was Alice. She said to me, "I'm sorry to disturb you, but I wanted to tell you right away that you must have made a mistake because you paid me too much." It turned out that I had given her an extra $20 bill by mistake.

I thanked her, of course, and asked her why she had decided to be so honest. She said to me, "Because it's the right thing to do. I would never want something like that on my conscience."

It's no wonder that Alice was a person who was completely comfortable with herself, self-assured and friendly. Part of the reason was that she had nothing to hide. Being ethical about being overpaid was simply an extension of her overall honesty and way of being. She would never have to wonder if being ethical was the right thing to do—it was automatic for her.

Ethical people have a natural sense of compassion for others. They would never do anything to harm someone else, certainly not intentionally. They would never kick someone when they are down or give themselves an unfair advantage by cheating or stealing. The implications of this type of behavior are *huge*. Consider this:

People who are ethical *rarely* have to feel bad about being mean, dishonest, or selfish. They have few regrets and almost never feel guilty. They feel comfortable trusting themselves because they trust their conscience. Others rely on them too because they are trustworthy. They don't live in fear or doubt about being caught or scrutinized because they live with integrity. In fact, they don't have to worry about what others think about them at all because they know in their hearts that they are doing the right thing. In any event, almost everyone thinks extremely well of them. Think of Alice for a moment. What's not to like?

If you dare to be ethical, it will be a decision you'll never regret. You'll live your life not believing but *knowing* that you're the best person you can be. You'll discover inner peace. You'll be proud of yourself and won't have to concern yourself with the negative consequences and implications of dishonesty or unethical behavior. You'll be free and happy.

# 45

# BECOME "BUTTON-PROOF"

One of the reasons so many people end up frustrated and stressed out by others is that they have their goals mixed up. If you desire a happy life, the idea is not to create a life where your buttons are never pushed. Instead, the goal is to create a state of mind where, even when your buttons are pushed, that's okay too because it won't get to you very much.

Let's face it. There are always going to be people who push your buttons. Most of the time it's going to be unintentional, but sometimes it's going to be on purpose. That shouldn't surprise you; it's just the way things are. Therefore, to insist that you'll be happy only when everyone starts to treat you exactly the way you would like to be treated—and to postpone your peace of mind until no one ever pushes your buttons—is an almost guaranteed way to remain stressed out for the rest of your life.

It's far wiser, I believe, and far more realistic to strive to become "button-proof." Can you imagine how great it would be to almost never get upset, annoyed, or bothered simply because someone was acting in a way that was inconsistent with your wishes? This doesn't mean you wouldn't prefer that people act in a certain way; we all do. It simply suggests that you would have the ability to brush things off, walk away, ignore, or dismiss potentially irritating comments, gestures, or behavior.

The way to make this happen for yourself is relatively easy. Instead of reacting to others as usual with resistance or repulsion, try to receive the things that usually seem bothersome with an attitude of acceptance. So, instead of saying to yourself, "Not again, I hate this," try looking at it differently. Instead, say to yourself, "Here's another chance to build my strength—here's another opportunity to not allow myself to become bothered."

You'll be amazed at how easy this strategy can be once you set your mind to it, because all it is, is a shift in your intention. Start with little things, like someone looking at you wrong or making a weird comment. Practice not getting mad; instead, dismiss it and let it go. If you fall into your old habit and become reactive, that's totally okay. It doesn't matter. You're going to lose it plenty of times during your lifetime—we all do. However, each time you succeed in letting something go instead of becoming upset, you become a little bit stronger and wiser, and you'll see the possibility of remaining calm and of "not sweating it."

Pretty soon, those same little things won't get to you very much, if at all. Then you'll be able to let even bigger things go, and so on. Like everything else, it just takes practice as well as the willingness to know exactly what you are practicing and why.

Remember, anyone can get angry and bothered by others—there's no trick to that. The secret is to know that true strength lies not in becoming irritated, as most people do, but in remaining calm, wise, and relatively unaffected when your buttons are being pushed.

# 46

# TRUST YOUR INNER SIGNALS

As a teen, you are fortunate to have an inner signal, a foolproof guidance system to let you know whether you are on track or off track. This "signal," which consists solely of your own feelings, lets you know whether you are headed toward stress, confusion, conflict, and other mental woes, or whether you are doing perfectly fine.

There is a powerful connection between your thinking and the way you feel. When we think, we immediately feel the effects of our thoughts. It happens in an instant. For example, if your goal was to get really angry right now, what would you have to do? The answer is, you'd have to think about something that makes you angry in order to feel angry. This suggests that if you're feeling jealous, it means you're having jealous thoughts. If you're feeling rushed, you're having hurried thoughts. If you're feeling happy, your thoughts are pleasant.

This is a powerful mental tool to have at your disposal. Let's assume, for example, that you're having a pretty nice day. Your feelings are pleasant, so, obviously, your thinking is working for you. No adjustment needs to be made. You just go on with your day. Later on, however, you begin to feel angry and frustrated.

Just like a inner buzzer that goes off in your mind, your feelings warn you that your thinking has become angry. No big deal. It's simply good information. Your feelings operate much like the warning lights on the dashboard of a car. They flash when trouble is brewing. They give you a heads-up that, if you continue driving, you might be moving toward some type of trouble.

Physical warning signals are easy to understand. If you have a sprained ankle, for example, the pain gives you information. It's telling you to stay off your ankle. It's telling you that now is *not* the time to be running or playing tennis.

In the same way, your feelings give you important information. If you're feeling angry, for example, your feelings tell you that your thinking has become angry. Rather than continue to think about everything that's making you angry, it might be wiser to recognize that you're having angry thoughts and back off a little. Take some time to clear your mind and take some deep breaths. Recognize that the anger is coming from inside of you—from those angry thoughts—not from the world. This is one of the toughest yet most important insights you can ever have. It will serve you in all aspects of your life. It will help you become less frustrated and help you stop sweating the small stuff.

This isn't to suggest that it's bad or wrong to feel anger, sadness, frustration, or anything else. Nor does it suggest that your anger or other feelings aren't justified, or that there aren't plenty of things to be mad about. It only means that your feelings (whatever they happen to be) are your guide. They tell you whether what is happening right now in your mind is productive or counterproductive, good for you or bad for you, and whether what is happening in this moment, within your own thoughts, is heading toward where you want to be—at peace, happy, and successful—or toward something else—frustration, stress, and conflict.

In my opinion, this is one of the most important mental dynamics you can ever become aware of. I use it all the time as a tool to let me know when I'm in need of a mental adjustment of some kind. Your feelings tell you with unbelievable accuracy how you are doing in any given moment. Trust them and what they are trying to tell you. If you do, you'll keep yourself on track most of the time.

# 47

# TAKE TIME OUT TO
# WATCH THE SUNSET

A cynic might say, "Oh right, that will be really helpful, especially to a teen," or "Could you be more superficial?" But do you know what? They're wrong. The truth is, many of the most powerful things you can do to improve your life are also very simple—and free.

When you learn to take time out to observe nature's beauty—sunset, sunrise, falling rain or snow, or a beautiful plant—on a regular basis, you are training yourself to slow down ever so slightly and appreciate life, beginning with the beauty around you. Like everything else, the more you do something, the better you become at it. If you keep it up, pretty soon you'll start noticing other aspects of life that are pretty special too. Indeed, when your life is filled with gratitude, everything looks less threatening and difficult. You spend less time irritated or wishing things were different and more time enjoying yourself and your day-to-day life.

The result is that, over time, rather than taking life quite as much for granted, you'll reexperience the magic of life. And when this happens, you'll be far less inclined, or even tempted, to search for artificial or harmful ways to create this magic. You won't need them because you'll already have it.

But that's not the only reason to take time out (every day) to watch the sunset. As you take time out to observe and appreciate the beauty in life, not only will you feel happier and more nourished, but others around you will be influenced by your attitude as well. By way of example, it's as if you give permission to others to do the same thing.

I asked seventeen-year-old Jessica to take a few extra minutes a day to go out of her way to appreciate beauty—the sunset or some other type of nature. She reported back to me that within a few days, her family life had become noticeably calmer. Her parents, even her kid brother, started by asking her what she was doing and, very quickly, began following her lead and taking time out themselves.

What seems to happen is that as "the appreciation factor" kicks in, the stress in the entire household is reduced. For a moment, everyone is calm, perhaps silent. Perspective is enhanced. There is less rushing around and less frantic behavior. The appreciation acts as a kind of reset button, giving everyone a fresh start. When business as usual resumes a minute or two later, the atmosphere is more balanced.

I hope you'll start this strategy right away. You'll love the beauty you're going to see as well as the way it makes you feel.

# 48

# READ A MINIMUM OF
# EIGHT PAGES A DAY

A friend and mentor of mine once gave me, as a gift, a huge collection of books by the same author. While I appreciated the gesture, the twenty-six volumes were quite intimidating to me. But as I opened the first book, he had inscribed a message that turned out to be one of the most valuable insights I have ever incorporated into my life. It said: "Becoming smart doesn't happen overnight. Read just eight pages a day, and you'll get through this stack in less than three years."

It hit me like a ton of bricks. To read eight pages only takes a few minutes but, cumulatively over many years, it really adds up. If you were to read a minimum of eight pages each day over a single year, that would add up to almost 3,000 pages. In ten years that number would skyrocket to almost 30,000!

Obviously, I'm talking about a minimum of eight pages above and beyond any required reading you have through school or other courses you might be taking. And newspapers, magazines, or browsing the Internet don't count. The reading I'm talking about is quiet, additional reading that is just for you. It can be a book designed to help you in some way such as this one, or it can be a book that is just for fun. I keep a stack of books next to my bed. I usually read a little before bed and again early in the morning. Some people like to read one book, start to finish, before going on. Others, like me, like to tackle six or eight at a time, switching back and forth depending on what seems most interesting on that day.

Many people find that, once they get into the habit, eight pages turns into eighteen and sometimes much more than that. Reading does that to you. The more you read, the more you learn to love it. But because I was helped so much by the eight-page minimum, I like to keep that number as a starting point.

I used to hate it when people would say to me "Reading is a gift." And you may hate me saying it to you, but I will anyway! Reading *is* a gift. It's something you can do almost anytime and anywhere. It can be a tremendous way to learn, relax, and even escape. So, enough about the virtues of reading. Time to read on.

# 49

# MAKE SPACE IN YOUR HEART
# FOR THOSE REALLY BAD DAYS

Everyone has bad days. Sometimes they are really bad. I've found that making space in your heart for those really bad days helps to keep them in perspective and to make them seem more manageable.

Making space in your heart for those really bad days involves learning to expect that, every once in a while, you're going to have one. It means making allowances for the fact that, while no one likes them, really bad days happen to all of us. No one is spared or exempt.

On the surface, it might seem that when you expect an occasional really bad day, you would be planting a negative seed, setting yourself up, or being pessimistic, but that's not really the case. When you expect something that is inevitable and built into the human experience, you're not being negative but rather accepting. And, the nice thing is, acceptance is at the root of not sweating the small stuff.

Being accepting of an occasional really bad day is no different from being accepting of an occasional rainy day. Most of us don't freak out when we see rain; instead, we accept it. We make allowances. We might not prefer it, but we accept it. Same thing with a really bad day. Rather than freaking out or thinking it's the end of the world, we can say to ourselves, "Oh well, it was inevitable. I'm glad it doesn't happen very often," or something like that. Often that little bit of perspective, and maybe even a tiny bit of humor, keeps you from making things even worse or thinking that things are worse than they are. Without acceptance, it's easy to convince yourself that "this always happens" and that your life is somehow falling apart.

Kelly said that when she was eighteen years old, she had what she believed was the "worst day of her life." Among the horrible things she experienced that day were that her mom's car was hit in the school parking lot, and her backpack, which contained the only copy of her research paper, was stolen. She said that her desire to not sweat the small stuff, along with her acceptance of the fact that everyone has an occasional horrible day, saved her sanity. While she wouldn't wish a day like that one on her worst enemy, she was able to recognize that, as bad as it was, things could have been much worse. No one was hurt in the accident, and she could re-create her paper in less time than it took to write it the first time. She said that keeping her cool enabled her to get through the day and deal with each problem as effectively as possible.

Embracing this strategy won't prevent you from having an occasional really bad day, but it will help you remember that even bad days will end, to be replaced, it is hoped, by much better days.

# 50

# DON'T SWEAT THE FUTURE

I met Noko during a book signing event. I remember her so well because her concerns almost broke my heart and because her "turnaround" brought me such joy.

In essence, Noko was in turmoil because she didn't yet know what she wanted to do with the rest of her life. She was panicked that she didn't know if she would make it into college or what kind of career she would have. She was insecure about whether she'd be able to make enough money, please her mom, or find the right husband. In short, she was immobilized because she felt she was running out of time and she didn't have any answers. And she was only fifteen!

We talked briefly about taking life one day at a time and about the power of making each day the best it can be. I remember saying to her, "Noko, *today* is the most important day of your life. By treating *each* day as the *most* important day, your future will automatically take care of itself." While it's certainly true we must plan for the future, it's counter-productive to worry too much about it.

It seems to me that one of the biggest mistakes most of us make is assuming that, for whatever reasons, tomorrow is going to be more important than today. What a silly assumption! Today is real. We are here today, and there are things we can do. There is no such guarantee with regard to tomorrow. In fact, tomorrow is a thought in our mind.

To me, it's always been reassuring to know that I guarantee my best possible future by making today all it can be. I believe the same is true for you too. This realization seems to take away the urgency and fear associated with not knowing what's going to happen. In fact, making the decision to do your best today actually makes not knowing exactly what's going to happen sort of exciting. You know it's going to work out well and you know you'll be fine—you just don't know the exact form it's going to take.

It's logical that if I do my best today with today's set of circumstances—and then I do the same thing again tomorrow, and then again the next day, and so forth—I'm setting myself up and planting the seeds for a great future. The decisions I make and the actions I take today will be the best I can do right now. I'll do the same thing tomorrow and next week and next year. Those "best I can do" decisions will add up and, eventually, will make up my future. In other words, someday today's "future" will be yet another "today." And when it arrives, my suggestion is to make it the best possible day.

About a year later I received a beautiful letter from Noko stating that while she still didn't know what she was going to do with her life when she was older, her concerns about it were all but over. She said that she had learned to be happy and that the past year was the best year of her life—not because her circumstances were any better or her future was any more secure, but simply because she had made the decision to do her best every day and let the future take care of itself.

I have no idea what Noko's future holds, but I do have absolute confidence that she will make a significant contribution to society and that her life will be filled with joy. The same will be true for you if you do your best—but don't sweat the future.

# 51

# EXPERIENCE VIBRANT HEALTH

I'm not a doctor or a nutritionist, yet I have experienced the joy of vibrant health. This strategy is a reminder of the importance and power of good physical health—and of doing everything you can to take care of yourself.

As a teen, you have a remarkable advantage: youth and vibrancy. Your body is young and strong. Unfortunately, however, many teens minimize this gift by filling their bodies with junk food and failing to get adequate exercise. This is sort of like putting heavy ankle weights on a champion athlete. The result is that you end up feeling just "okay" rather than fantastic.

As you know, being a teen can be pretty tough. Feeling just "okay" doesn't make things any easier. Can you imagine, however, the edge you would have and how much easier life might seem if, instead of feeling "okay," you felt great?

There is something incredible, almost magical, about feeling as good as you are able to feel. As a teen, that good physical feeling is potentially remarkable. But it does take some discipline.

What do you think about trying to become as healthy as possible as an experiment? You can start by learning everything you can about nutrition and exercise. Visit the library. Read books and health-related magazines. Next, talk to your doctor and come up with a plan that seeks to maximize your physical health. Find out from an expert if there are foods that you're eating that may be contributing to a lack of energy and vitality, anxiety, depression, or mood swings. See if there are foods or vitamins that you could be consuming that might add to your physical health. Ask about how exercise might increase your sense of well-being, which, in my mind, translates into optimism and happiness.

What have you got to lose? I can't imagine that trying to be healthier would do any harm. You'll look and feel great. You will have boundless energy and enthusiasm. You'll be strong and healthy. And who knows? Maybe when you're feeling better physically, you won't be sweating the small stuff as much anymore either.

# 52

# VISIT THE ELDERLY

I read about Steve, a fourteen-year-old who spent an hour a week visiting elderly people in a nursing home. In the article he said that he did so not so much for the residents of the home, but for himself. He said he learned so much that his visits had become a treasured part of his week. I was so impressed with what he had to say that I began asking around, to see if others were doing the same. I discovered that many teens from around the world love to spend time with elderly people for a variety of reasons. Some do so because the people they visit love and appreciate their company; others do so for the gifts they receive.

Elderly people often have a younger, happier, and wiser spirit than people much younger in actual years. Many times they are much more patient, accepting, humorous, and nonjudgmental, and far better listeners. Very often they have amazing stories to share and invaluable information based on actual life experience. Sometimes even very old people who can no longer speak very well, or who are confined to a bed or wheelchair, have a loving, gentle, and special presence that is nourishing to be around.

My grandmother, who died a few years ago, lived in a nursing home the last year of her life. I loved visiting her and having the opportunity simply to sit in her presence. We didn't need to say anything, just to hold hands. I also enjoyed visiting with several of the other residents in her home. They had accumulated such wisdom and were so willing to share. I found myself asking for advice and learning a great deal. After all, these were people with up to three times my life experience!

If you wanted to learn to drive a car, you'd visit a driving instructor. If you wanted to learn to play basketball, you'd spend time with a coach or other players. The same is true with virtually anything you'd like to learn about. You probably would choose to spend time and energy with someone with experience.

My suggestion is this: If you want to learn about life, spend at least some time with those people who have the most life experience: the elderly. Doing this might involve visiting your grandparents or other people's grandparents on a regular basis. Or you might have elderly neighbors who would love your company. Or you might choose to visit people in a nursing home, retirement center, or some type of community center. If you ask around, you'll find the perfect people to visit.

And when you do, ask plenty of questions and really listen to what the people have to say. It's a great way to enrich your own life, brighten the lives of those you visit, and learn some incredible things. If you take this step, it just might become a very important part of your life.

# 53

# BE AWARE OF THE LAW
# OF DIMINISHING RETURNS

The law of diminishing returns says that, while there are many great things in life, some of them have less and less value the more you do them. At some point, in fact, the value or benefit disappears and the activity begins to work against you.

Some obvious examples: It can be fun to stay up really late, but without some sleep, you become so tired that you ruin the experience. A chocolate sundae may be delicious, but eating three of them might make you sick. Having friends is one of the greatest gifts of life, but if you had a hundred good friends, you wouldn't be able to keep track of them. It's great to use the Internet, but what would happen to your life if you did nothing else?

One of my personal favorite examples is drinking coffee. I love to have a cup, maybe even two. But if I drink much more than that, I begin to feel agitated and hyper. Taken to an extreme, I'd become a nervous wreck.

You can extend the same idea to the mental aspects of life. It's probably important, for example, that you're able to identify flaws and weaknesses. Yet if you do this too much, that's all you'll see. You'll end up disappointed, unhappy, and stressed out. But as soon as you're able to identify a behavior as being subject to the law of diminishing returns, you can eliminate this problem because you'll know better when to back off.

I was talking to a teen about this very issue regarding his parents. Specifically, he said, "I've learned that negotiating with my parents is a good thing to do. However, at some point, if I push too hard, it's predictable that they will begin to feel badgered. They will then shut down and all my efforts begin to work against me." He was learning the delicate art of knowing when to back off and soften. Without this skill, life with parents and everyone else becomes adversarial.

I try to use the same logic when parenting my kids. Obviously, I have to teach them certain things—but I also try to recognize when my good intentions become yet another lecture! Or, when a friend asks for advice, I try to know when enough is enough. It's all about finding that line—knowing when to pursue something and when it's time to relax about it or try something new. It's also about knowing when something isn't working well and perhaps when it's time to try a new approach.

This understanding has been immensely helpful in my life and in the lives of many others. I hope you'll give it some careful consideration, because it can assist you in preventing many of the most stress-creating habits in life.

## 54

# DEVELOP YOUR PRESENCE

There's something truly special about people who have "presence." It's that magical, almost magnetlike quality that makes you want to be around someone. When you're around someone who has presence, it's nourishing, refreshing, and fun. You feel special, listened to, and respected, almost as if you're the most important person in the world.

Developing your own presence does essentially two things. First, because it's linked to being present moment–oriented, it reduces your stress and makes you happier. Instead of wandering all over the place, your mind is focused on exactly what you're doing or whom you are with. This frees your mind from the distractions of worry, negativity, and regret. Being present allows your mind to rest, to become focused, attentive, and peaceful. Developing your presence will make you more patient and less reactive—and, ultimately, much smarter and wiser. Your learning curve will sharpen, and life will become more interesting and less frustrating.

Second, developing your presence will improve *all* of your relationships—romantic ones as well as those with your parents, teachers, siblings, employers, friends, even strangers. The stronger your presence, the more you'll bring out the best in others and the more they will want to be with you and to help you. Obviously, this will help reduce your stress even further and will make your life a great deal easier.

It's easy and natural to be "present" when you are in love with or very interested in someone. Because you can't seem to get enough of that person, you're highly attentive. Your ability to remain attentive feeds on itself and brings you even closer together. In other words, *your* presence is nourishing to the other person, which in turn feeds his or her need to be listened to and respected. This feeling makes that person want to be around you even more. Communication is heightened on both ends, and everyone wins.

Where it gets tricky is when you don't feel as motivated to be "right there" with someone, say when you're talking to a parent or teacher, when you're feeling lectured to or when you're discussing things that put you to sleep. Yet this is the time your efforts will pay the highest dividends.

The best way to develop your presence is to see what's in it for you; the answer is an easier life and better relationships. The rest is pretty easy; all it takes is practice. Try to immerse yourself in what you're doing and simply notice when your mind drifts away. When it does, gently bring it back. The same is true when you're with someone, whoever it is. Stay with the conversation and pay attention as best you can. As your mind wanders, simply call it back just as you would a little puppy who was wandering from home. Do this over and over again and it will become second nature.

Other people will notice the changes in you, and that will be nice. But what's even better is that you'll notice changes in yourself. I think you'll agree that many of the people you respect most in the world have a great deal of presence. These people also tend to have the most adventuresome, fun lives. There's no question that, if you put your mind to it, you can become this type of person. To do so may be one of the most important decisions you ever make.

## 55

# REMIND YOURSELF THAT
# NO ONE IS OUT TO GET YOU

I read a story that was forwarded to me over the Internet about a well-known celebrity. While I can't guarantee the accuracy of the story, I can tell you that it was very inspiring. Supposedly, someone had asked this man if there were some reason for the sudden change in his attitude, inspiration, and success. He said that, above all, he had come to the simple realization that no one was out to get him.

On the surface, this is an obvious observation. Most of us, if asked, would probably admit that few people, if anyone, are really out to get us. Yet many of us act as if there are people out there trying to do just that. We behave as if we have a chip on our shoulder, or we act suspicious, cynical, or paranoid. Or we act like victims, feeling sorry for ourselves when things don't go our way. We think it must be someone else's fault—it's not fair. This heavy-hearted attitude takes an enormous toll on our sense of well-being and our experience of life. It robs us of enthusiasm, inspiration, wisdom, creativity, follow-through, and spontaneity.

In order to have the "no one is out to get me" insight, all that is required is a willingness on your part to accept the fact that you're just like everyone else. Me too; I'm just like everyone else. The simple truth is that while we're all special and unique, none of us is important enough in the eyes of someone else to warrant that type of attention. You do hear isolated stories of stalkers and weirdos, but, truthfully, those are the rare exceptions. For most of us, when someone isn't nice to us—or they treat us unfairly, or do something we don't like, or say the wrong thing— it's really not about us. Or if it is, it's minimal.

Most people are simply going about their own business and doing the very best they can. And while people can and do hurt our feelings, usually it's by accident or it's some attempt to do something in their own self-interest. No one planned for us to be hurt or involved in a negative way. Ordinarily, fate or thoughtlessness or something like that caused the negative outcome.

Acknowledging the fact that no one is out to get us assists our creativity, persistence, responsibility, and willingness to take charge of our own lives. It will help you become a happier and more productive individual.

# 56

# GO THE EXTRA MILE

We've all heard it many times: "Give it your best shot." "Do your best." "Give a 100 percent effort." "Go the extra mile." Yet because we're not always sure what the "payoff" might be for our efforts, sometimes we adopt the attitude of "Why bother?"

I've found it to be extremely helpful to remember this: While I don't always know what my reward, if any, will be on any given project, I do know that when I give my best effort to whatever I'm working on, rewards often come from unexpected sources.

I received a story on my e-mail from an anonymous person that demonstrates this point extremely well.

An elderly carpenter was ready to retire. He told his employer-contractor of his plans to leave the house-building business and live a more leisurely life with his wife, enjoying his extended family. He would miss the paycheck, but he needed to retire. They could get by.

The contractor was sorry to see his good worker go and asked if he could build just one more house as a personal favor. The carpenter agreed, but in time it was easy to see that his heart was not in his work. He resorted to shoddy workmanship and used inferior materials. It was an unfortunate way to end a dedicated career.

When the carpenter finished his work, the employer came to inspect the house. He handed the front door key to the carpenter. "This is your house," he said. "My gift to you."

The carpenter was shocked. What a shame! If he had only known he was building his own house, he would have done it differently.

So it is with us. We build our lives, one day at a time, often putting less than our best effort into the building. Then with a shock we realize we have to live in the house we have built. If we could do it over, we'd do it much differently. But we cannot go back.

You are the carpenter. Each day you hammer a nail, place a board, or erect a wall. Your attitudes and the choices you make today build the "house" you live in tomorrow.

I couldn't have said it any better, and that's why I wanted to share this story with you.

As a teen, you have absolute control over the way you build the house of your future. You have your entire life in front of you. If you go the extra mile; give life your best shot; live with integrity, kindness, honesty, and thoughtfulness; then, chances are, you're going to build a real beauty; a house you can be proud of.

# 57

# WATCH YOUR LANGUAGE

Don't worry, I'm not giving you a lecture on the evils of a foul mouth. What I mean by watching your language is to become aware that the words you choose to express yourself with, and the things you choose to talk about, play an important role in the overall quality of your life.

I once asked two teenage brothers to try the following experiment, just for fun. I asked them to try to go an entire day without swearing, criticizing, or any talk of anything having to do with violence, sex, or greed.

The first time they tried it, they couldn't do it! They told me that within an hour they had failed the test several times. I reminded them that in this experiment there is no such thing as failure. In fact, it was great that they couldn't do it because it showed them just how much of what they said was geared toward things that did not necessarily promote happiness.

They went back for round two and did much better than before. In fact, what they learned was so eye-opening to them that I decided to ask you to do the same thing. I asked them to think back on that day and tell me what they remembered most. What stood out for each of them was that their spirits were much higher than usual—they were happier.

It's interesting to try this experiment and to observe that, when you do so, it's very difficult to have a bad day. The reason is that your word choices are very closely related to what you are thinking about and focused upon. So the act of watching your language gears your attention on other topics and aspects of life.

If you think about it, the reverse would also be true. Imagine (but don't try this) if the exercise was to go an entire day in which you were only allowed to swear, criticize others, and discuss violence, sex, or greed. Imagine how you would feel. It would be virtually impossible to have a good day!

What this exercise tends to do, beyond the initial experiment, is to get you thinking about the power of your own words. What tends to happen is that people become a little more careful of what they talk about. They start to equate peaceful feelings with peaceful speech.

The idea isn't to be perfect or to never, ever discuss anything negative or having to do with sex, violence, or greed. That would be putting your head in the sand. Instead, simply experiment with paying closer attention to what you say and talk about—watch your language a little more carefully.

## 58

# BE CREATIVE
# IN YOUR REBELLION

I've not met many teens who weren't at least a little rebellious. I certainly was. My guess is that there isn't anything inherently dangerous or wrong with rebellion, in and of itself. The problem is most often the *form* that the rebellion takes.

At the risk of sounding corny, I'm going to suggest that the ultimate form of rebellion—one that is both effective and healthy—is to make the decision to be happy. That's right, to be happy. And, while you're at it, to be satisfied and content.

Think about it. The media and the advertisers want you to believe that you *can't* be happy unless you buy their products and are influenced by their programming. They want you to believe that you need to look a certain way, dress a certain way, think a certain way, even smell a certain way. You need specific skin products, certain types of clothes, makeup, perfume, and hair care products. Of course, you need expensive shoes and to look like a supermodel or body builder too. Otherwise, you shouldn't feel good about yourself. How could you?

And do you know what? As ridiculous as this seems, most teens (and most adults too) buy it, hook, line, and sinker! Almost everyone seems to believe that they can't be happy unless they have the right stuff and unless they look different. These beliefs encourage low self-esteem, unhappiness, hopelessness, and a lack of contentment. As an adult, these types of beliefs often turn into "I can't be happy unless my life is different from what it is—my circumstances need to change."

Make no mistake about it: Encouraging you to be discontented is a huge business. These companies not only want, they *need* for you to be insecure and unhappy. If you become content, their reason for being ceases to exist. If you don't need them anymore, they will be out of business. So, what better way to be rebellious than to try to do just that—fight back! Avoid being the way so many people are—serious, uptight, selfish, needy, and insecure—and become happy with who you are and with what you have now.

I've taken on this philosophy in my own life. It's great fun to put it into practice, to see how happy you can be without buying in to the "you have to be different (and have different things)" trap. It's amazing how the simple decision to be happy translates into a better life and a more powerful, optimistic attitude. Once you decide to be happy, you'll find yourself thinking happy thoughts and dismissing ones that aren't. You'll automatically become more confident because you'll know that you don't really need those products, and you don't really need to dress differently or be thinner or whatever—others just wanted you to believe that you did.

So, my suggestion is this: Go ahead and be rebellious—*really* rebellious. Do something most others wouldn't dare: Be happy. You'll be different, and you'll have the last laugh.

# 59

# LET PEOPLE TALK

I'd like to discuss a strategy that's a virtually guaranteed way to succeed. I'm referring here to the simple act of letting people talk. Almost all people love to talk more than they love to listen. And even people who are shy or who don't talk too much usually do love to talk once they feel comfortable and get going. The icing on the cake is when people are not only allowed to talk, but when they feel listened to and aren't interrupted!

For whatever reasons, human beings seem to have an instinctual need to be heard. When that need isn't met, people feel as if something is missing. There is an emptiness of some kind. When that need is met, however, people often feel nourished and satisfied. If you can think of people who really listen to what you are saying—and who don't interrupt you—my guess is that you are very fond of them. If you can't think of anyone, you're not alone.

I've asked many teens if they feel "really listened to," and, not surprisingly, very few have said yes. It's a fairly safe bet that most of the people you come into contact with will answer the same way. They too feel as if no one (or at least very few people) let them talk without interrupting them.

This being the case, what do you suppose will happen when *you* become the person who lets people talk? Without being too dramatic about it, you'll be unique—you'll become a hero! As your listening skills increase, and as you let others talk, people will feel comfortable around you. They will feel nourished and heard. They will trust you. Even though people may not know what it is about you, most of them will like you.

When people know that you are sincere and that you genuinely care about them and that you are interested in what they have to say, they will be on your side and will want to see you succeed. They will want to help you or, at very least, be nice to you. They also will be more interested in hearing what *you* have to say. One of the keys to great relationships is making sure you let each other talk—and that you both listen.

Obviously, you would never let someone talk only because you want him or her to like you. To do so would be lacking in sincerity. Being liked is a result, a perk, of letting people talk. You want to let people talk primarily because doing so is polite and thoughtful—and because making other people happy will help to make you happy. When you listen well and let others talk, everyone ends up a winner.

# 60

# REFLECT ON THE MAP

Compassion plays an enormous role in your becoming a more peaceful and happy person. When you are aware of—and when you care about—people all over this beautiful planet and what they are going through, you feel connected to others and your own problems are put into perspective.

When I suggest reflecting on the map, I'm advising people to become at least a little bit aware of the plight of people all around the world. By becoming if not involved, at least aware of the hunger, violence, poverty, hopelessness, wars, disease, drought, famine, and other serious problems that exist, you become more philosophical about what you yourself are going through, whatever that might be. Rather than being zeroed in on your own concerns and problems, you expand your vision to encompass the rest of humanity.

Another way to look at it is this: Imagine your own problems shoved up against your face—right there in front of you at all times. Now imagine how relieved you'd be if you simply could put some distance between yourself and those problems. The problems would still be there; they would just look a tiny bit less intense and intimidating. That's exactly what happens to your perception of your problems when you become aware of the problems of others.

All of us are born into a certain set of circumstances, and it's unrealistic to think that you're ever going to get to a point where you're never frustrated. Everyone gets frustrated, angry, down, anxious, and all the rest, regardless of his or her circumstances.

The idea of reflecting on the map is not to compare your situation with that of others and then feel guilty if your circumstances seem or are easier than someone else's. Nor is the idea to say to yourself, "Gee, my situation isn't so bad after all—I shouldn't ever get upset." Instead, the idea is to be grateful that you're in a position to be *able* to reflect on the map, that you're aware of what goes on around the world, and that you're able to feel compassion for others. In addition, becoming more aware of the hardships around the globe reminds you, vividly, that everyone has problems—many far more serious than our own. This added bit of perspective doesn't minimize what you're going through, nor does it suggest that your life isn't difficult. It *is* difficult. Yet this viewpoint does allow you to keep everything in better perspective. And perspective is a powerful tool in the game of life.

Everyone I know who spends time reflecting on the map has become a more grateful and compassionate person. Often these people are able to let go of little things far more easily than before. In addition, they are almost always drawn to do something, however small, to be of help. Simply spending a little time and energy thinking about why we should be grateful makes us realize how small the world really is and how unnecessary it is to sweat the small stuff.

# 61

# DISH OUT PRAISE

We've previously discussed the fact that encouraging people to like you reduces stress. There's no question that life is easier and less stressful when people want to see you succeed, trust you, are on your side, treat you well, and like you.

If I had to choose something that almost everyone loves, it would be difficult not to consider "receiving genuine praise" at or near the top of the list. I don't think I've ever met anyone who doesn't love to receive compliments and praise, so long as they're real.

While it's fairly obvious that dishing out genuine praise is a great idea, it's surprising how few people do it. There seem to be several reasons for this. Some people are too shy to deliver praise; it makes them feel uncomfortable. Others feel that people "don't need praise" or that they already know how wonderful they are. Some simply haven't recognized how important praising others really is.

While overcoming these or other objections might be difficult, it's nevertheless worth the effort. The truth is, most people feel they don't get nearly enough praise and could always use (and would love to receive) more.

On several occasions, I've given someone a genuine compliment from my heart, someone later has told me that that person thought I was wonderful and kind. How could they possibly feel that way, given that we had only spent a minute or two together? I wondered. Then it hit me—I had given the person a genuine compliment from my heart. That's the power of dishing out praise.

When I think of the kindest people I know, all of them are in the habit of dishing out praise and compliments. It's hard *not* to like someone who is in the habit of praising others. Think about the people in your life who have given you genuine compliments. Who are they? Do you like them? Now think of the people whom you have given praise to. I'll bet they like you too.

Eighteen-year-old Stefanie told me that she had given her instructor a simple but genuine compliment. Specifically, she said, "You are very patient with your students, and I really appreciate that. It must be hard to work with so many people all at the same time. You do a really great job." When the school year was over and Stefanie had received an A, her teacher told her that she was the first student to give her such a nice, sincere compliment. The instructor appreciated it and remembered it. That simple praise had made her school year a little bit better. It's a good example of something really small making a really big difference.

A cynic would say Stefanie was kissing up. She wasn't; Stefanie really thought her teacher was doing a great job. Her instructor, being a human being, took a liking to Stefanie. She was willing to work with her after class and was always happy to answer her questions. She was on Stefanie's side and really wanted her to succeed. She didn't give her a good grade because of what Stefanie had said—but it sure didn't hurt.

Dishing out praise is one of those "intangibles" of life. There's no way to quantify exactly how much good it does—but we know it does a lot of good and that, as long as it's genuine, there's no downside. So when it's for real and deserved, explore the magic of praise. The more you do it, the more comfortable you'll become. My guess is, your life will suddenly seem easier—and now you'll know why.

# 62

# DON'T BURN BRIDGES

If your goal was to create a ton of unnecessary stress for yourself, one of my suggestions would be for you to burn as many bridges as possible. Burning bridges is a phrase that means interacting with people so as to ensure that they won't like you ever again and that they won't want anything to do with you ever again. It's like closing a door permanently.

A bridge represents a connection between you and the other side. If you burned a bridge, you would be eliminating a means of getting across. Likewise, when you burn a "human bridge," you're destroying your connection with another person, often forever.

There are many ways to burn bridges. One of the ways people do so happens when someone is mad at someone else. Rather than finding a constructive way to express that anger and work things out, a person overreacts and uses very strong, absolute statements: "I'll *never* talk to you again," "I've *always* hated you." Sometimes, as you can imagine, they say something even worse. People also can burn bridges by doing mean-spirited things to others and then compound the problem by failing to apologize. Whenever you wound people, offend them significantly, or seriously question their honor, you're risking the possibility of burning a bridge.

If you're aware of the importance of not burning bridges, you're more likely to avoid doing so. This awareness can help you bite your tongue when you might want to scream or overreact—and it can help you keep things in perspective when you're about to blow something way out of proportion. It also can help you walk away when you feel like fighting, or come up with a more creative way to get something off your chest.

One of my personal goals is to never burn any bridges. However, like everyone else, there have been times when I have been tremendously angry with someone. On more than one occasion I've written a very harsh letter to someone, expressing exactly how I feel. But rather than sending the letter, which probably would have burned a bridge, I've thrown the letter away. Then, after cooling down, I would either discuss the problem with or write the person again, this time using better judgment. The only thing that prevented me from burning the bridge was my awareness that burning bridges is generally a bad idea and a destructive thing to do. In fact, I can't think of anything good that could possibly come about as a result of a burned bridge.

The good news is, it's usually possible to restore a burned bridge with genuine humility. The key is to be willing to be the first one to act loving or to reach out. A sincere apology is a very powerful remedy and has a way of bridging the gap between even the most damaged "bridges." So, while it's never a good idea to burn a bridge and it's a good idea to try to never do so, if you do "start a fire," there's always the possibility to restore the connection.

# 63

# UNDERSTAND

# THE LAW OF FOCUS

Understanding the law of focus is, in my opinion, one of the most essential ingredients to a happy, relatively stress-free life. Luckily, it's also one of the easiest things in the world to grasp!

Here's all there is to it: *What you focus on expands in your mind.* It gets bigger. That's it.

Usually we think of focus as a good thing. And it is. Focus is similar to concentration; it's essential for learning and success. But for the purposes of this strategy, I want to discuss the potentially harmful side of focus and when to back off.

Think about what happens when you focus your attention on something that annoys you. Suppose, for example, someone offered you $20 if you could think of something about one of your teachers that bugs you. Could you do it? Of course you could. Go ahead and pick something. Think about it now. Think some more. Be specific. Imagine every detail.

Did you notice that the more you think about it, the bigger and more important it seems? The more you focus on something, the more significant it seems to become. That's why you hear stories about people getting annoyed with others who squeeze the toothpaste the wrong way, or something stupid like that. Obviously, there are few things less relevant than the way a tube of toothpaste is squeezed. Yet if you focus enough attention on it and you imagine the motivations behind it, pretty soon the toothpaste-squeezing starts to seem pretty important.

The same dynamic holds true with whatever bugs you. If you focus on the flaws of a friend long enough, you'll begin to question why he or she is your friend at all. If you focus on a mistake you made—give it too much attention—you'll begin to feel bad about yourself. Focusing on little things turns them into big things. This is one of the key reasons why people sweat the small stuff! Some small thing happens and they zero in on it, focus on it too much, and turn it into a really big deal.

Does this mean it's never appropriate to get upset? Absolutely not! All it suggests is that your focus is a contributing factor that can turn a minor annoyance into something much bigger.

Suppose you're in line and someone cuts in front of you. Is it OK to feel annoyed? Of course, but it's a question of degree. You can feel a little annoyed and you might even say something to the person, if it seems important, and then let it go. On the other hand, if you focus on it too much, you can, very easily, blow it out of proportion. That's what people do when they fight over things like that. In and of itself, someone cutting in line is just that—someone cutting in line. It's our focus on that event that turns it into a really big deal.

Whenever you start to feel annoyed, bothered, or irritated, it's a good idea to come back to the law of focus. Remind yourself that your own degree of focus is contributing, in a big way, to how you're feeling. This doesn't mean it's wrong to feel angry, sad, or annoyed. It only means that if your goal is to be less angry, sad, or annoyed, it's helpful to acknowledge the power of focus. When you do, the world seems to be less upsetting to us—and we seem to have more control in our lives.

# 64

# USE REMINDER CARDS

This is a strategy I've used for many years. Using reminder cards has proven again and again to be a simple yet powerful way to remind myself of certain important points.

Most of us have very good intentions when it comes to our own mental health and happiness. For the most part, we know what type of thoughts and actions will bring about happiness, as well as which ones will do the opposite. The problem is, we're so busy living our lives, solving problems, attending to our responsibilities, and interacting with other people that we sometimes forget to remind ourselves and therefore implement the ideas that will make our lives peaceful, productive, and happy.

Reminder cards are a great way to have the reminding done for us. They are free, since you make them yourself. On a plain flash card or small piece of paper, simply write down any thoughts, ideas, or insights that are particularly meaningful to you. Then keep them in places where you're likely to see and refer to them—a backpack, car visor, purse or wallet, inside a book, next to your bed, etc. What you write on the cards themselves can be either a positive, life-affirming statement or a question that is designed to remind you of an important idea.

Here are a few examples of reminder cards that I've used: "Am I experiencing the power of love and forgiveness today?" "Life isn't an emergency." "I can choose happiness." "I will look for the good and beauty in everything around me." "Have I told someone close to me how much I love her recently?" and "Start to see the innocence in everybody." I could go on and on, but I'm sure you get the idea. Your reminder cards might be similar to mine, or entirely different. It depends on what you'd like to emphasize—success, happiness, overcoming adversity, kindness, compassion, grades, friendships, or whatever else.

Using these cards is one of the simplest ideas in this book, yet it really does work. Reminder cards remind you of what you already know and reinforce that which you deem important. Start using them today, and I'm sure you'll notice a positive change right away.

# 65

# BE GLAD TO BE A TEEN

We live in a strange world. When you're young, you're encouraged to grow up really fast. Then, as you get older, you're encouraged to do everything humanly possible to stay young!

Being a teen is cool. You're exactly the age you need to be. You're already a young adult. Enjoy it while you can. Despite the fact that everyone is trying to force you to grow up really fast, there's no need to "buy in" all the way. You'll be an adult a lot longer than you'll be a teen. The reason that so few people are happy is that they are preoccupied with being something that they're not. Very few people are satisfied with where they are; most perceive something else or somewhere else as better. Once you decide that today, right where you are, is good enough, you'll begin to make the most of the life that you have. You'll make great decisions about your future without sacrificing the joys of your younger years.

One of my favorite cartoons pictured two guys who were ready to walk into a formal cocktail party full of people. The caption read, "Yipes, grown-ups!" I laughed because that's the way I feel so much of the time, even though I'm one of them.

So many people, particularly adults, see life as serious business. Everything is an emergency or a contest. People are uptight, in a hurry, take themselves too seriously, are highly stressed, and lacking in gratitude.

Whenever I find myself getting too stressed out, I remind myself that life is an incredible gift. Each day, in fact, is special and unique; none is more important than the others. We are here for a parenthesis in eternity. Why not spend less time and energy wishing we were somewhere else and more time and energy making each day all it can be?

I've been asked, more than once, "Are you suggesting that life isn't hard or that you don't need to work hard?" My answer has always been, "Of course not." Life is often very hard, and the only way I know of to get through it is to work hard. But you can work hard, achieve, do your best, compete, pursue dreams, contribute, give back, and all the rest without becoming a stressed-out, burned-out monster. You can do all these things and more while still keeping your perspective, having fun, and being ethical and thoughtful. The first step in having it all is to like who you are right now. Be glad you're a teen!

# 66

# EXPERIENCE

# DEEP LISTENING

So often when we're listening, a variety of other things are going on at the same time. Either we're preoccupied with other thoughts, or we're secretly awaiting our turn to talk. Either way, our minds are busy thinking of other things at the same moment we are trying to listen.

Other times we're comparing what we are hearing to what we already know or believe. So, we're either agreeing or disagreeing with what is being said. If we agree with a statement, we tend to think something like, "I already know that." If we disagree, we think to ourselves, "No, that's not right." Again, either way, our minds are "filled up" while we're listening.

This "busy" or "surface" listening is, by far, the most common type of day-to-day listening. Yet because it's so distracting, it's highly ineffective. It causes stress, relationship problems, confusion, and a poor learning curve.

Have you ever been trying to sleep when a pesky mosquito was zooming around your ear? If so, you've experienced the frustration of trying to relax with a noise-related distraction. You can't relax fully because your attention is scattered. The buzzing of the insect is irritating to your senses and interferes with what you are trying to do.

Imagine that you were trying to have an intimate conversation with someone while at the same time someone else was sitting next to you, yelling in your ear. Needless to say, it would be difficult to enjoy your conversation. Like the mosquito, the voice would be an irritant and a huge distraction.

Now imagine that the mosquito and the yelling person were suddenly taken out of the picture. In both examples, all of a sudden your ability to concentrate, relax, and enjoy would be enhanced. Likewise, your stress would go away.

In the same way, when you listen "deeply," with a clear mind, you create an environment for a rich and fulfilling experience. When you listen with nothing on your mind, you open yourself to a world of new opportunities—with other people, in learning, in relaxing, and in your enjoyment.

With deep listening, you receive information in its purest form without the distraction and stress of internal noise (thoughts). You are able to hear what is being said as it is intended. Your relationships will improve too. When people are talking to you, they will sense your deep and sincere listening; therefore, they will feel as if you are hearing them. Your sincere listening will enhance your connection as people will love to talk to you. They will feel understood and respected.

It's relatively easy to experience deep listening. All you need to do is to understand its importance and to give it some practice. But it's not "practice" in the way we sometimes think of practice. There's little effort involved. In fact, the less effort you expend, the easier it will be. What you want to do is clear your mind and relax—but at the same time, really be there with the other person. By doing this you're removing the distractions.

As you listen, notice how your mind tends to fill with other things—plans, answers, ideas, questions, fears, fantasies, whatever. When this happens, gently clear your mind and simply listen. While the person is talking, try not to judge, evaluate, agree, or disagree with what is being said, or think of anything else, until he is finished. Simply absorb what is being said. Listen fully and deeply.

Because this type of listening is so rewarding, likely you will be highly motivated to keep it up. Although it will become easier and easier over time, be patient with yourself. It takes some time to break old habits. Don't worry; even slight improvements in your deep listening skills will reap nice rewards. One final note: As you get better at this type of listening, try to be patient with others. Be aware that it's likely that they too could use some practice in deep listening.

# 67

# BE WARY OF FRIENDS
# WHO ENCOURAGE YOU TO DWELL

There's an important distinction to be made between a friend who listens well and one who simply encourages you to dwell on things. Obviously, a good friend who listens well is one of life's greatest gifts and joys. Those of us who are fortunate enough to have such friends are lucky indeed. A good listener is someone who really cares about you and wants to see you happy. She feels your pain but also shares in your joy.

Sometimes, however, someone can appear, on the surface, to be a good listener but is actually more concerned with encouraging you to dwell on your problems and the things that bug you. It can be tricky to tell because someone can seem to listen well when she says things like, "Tell me more," or, "That's terrible, doesn't it bug you?" When you look more closely, however, you'll notice that a vast majority of the questions and comments from these people are specifically geared to keep you caught up and zeroed in on the things that are upsetting you. One way to tell is that you sweat the small stuff more, not less, after being around such people.

The reason it's important to determine the difference is that certain people thrive on hearing about other people's problems. It's one of the ways they feel alive and important. In addition, it's a way that some people justify their own feelings of anger or frustration. In other words, if they can keep you caught up and focused on your problems and concerns, they feel that their own confused feelings are justified. The more you stay upset, the better they feel about things. More often than not, they're not even aware they are doing this—but nevertheless, it's hurtful to you when it happens. An eighteen-year-old guy recently shared with me that his decision to spend less time with what he called "the energy drainers" was the single most positive decision he had made in years. It freed up energy and happiness that he didn't even know he had.

You have to wonder what the motivation could be when someone is constantly firing questions to you such as, "Doesn't that irritate you?"or statements like, "I'd never put up with that." It's almost as if these people are personally invested in seeing you become upset—or in keeping you down once you are. True friends will listen to your concerns, of course, but always seem to have an interest in helping you climb back up again as well. They have compassion for the problems you face, but receive no joy in hearing about them.

I'm not suggesting that you start analyzing the motives of your friends and other people. Please know that an occasional question that brings you down doesn't mandate the termination of a friendship! I'm referring only to people who do this routinely, as part of their normal way of being with you. People are free to choose their own friends, and do so for many reasons. I hope you'll try to hang around people who truly have your best interests at heart—as you do for them.

## 68

# CREATE YOUR OWN
# SPECIAL PLACE

Since I'm a very private person who loves solitude, this strategy has particular meaning for me. Going to my own special place, just to be alone and quiet, has become one of the greatest joys of my life. Each minute I'm there seems to have the power to release any amount of stress that I had been experiencing.

Having your own special place can serve many important functions. It's a place where you can be alone to think or reflect. It's a place where you can pray or meditate, draw or write poetry, or write in your journal. It's a place where you can clear your mind and be still. But more important than what you do while you're there, the best and perhaps most important part is that you associate your special place with peace and happiness.

Although many people long for their own special place, some fear it's unrealistic because of financial reasons. Finances don't have to be an obstacle. I know, because I had my own special place, even as a kid. Your place doesn't have to be an entire room. It can be a corner of a room, under a set of stairs, or part of a closet. If need be, it can even be outside. In fact, my older daughter has a special place in the yard she calls her fort. She goes there when she wants to be alone or when she feels the need to escape chaos. Once I entered without her permission, not knowing she was there. Immediately, in a firm but loving tone, she asked me to leave.

There are no rules about having a special place, such as how often you visit or how long you should stay once you're there. It doesn't matter what it looks like either. You can decorate it or not; it's up to you. The only thing that's important is that you think of it as your own—a place to go when you feel like being alone.

I've found that when I'm feeling happy, being in my special place enhances and deepens that feeling. When I'm uptight and sweating the small stuff, it helps me relax and regain my perspective. When I'm sad, it helps me clear my mind and get back on track. And when I feel like I just need some space from others, it's the perfect place to get away.

You might want to look around and see what might work for you. If you love what you find, great, stick with it. But if it doesn't feel right, don't worry. In time you'll find the best possible place for you.

# 69

# REMEMBER TO BE GRATEFUL

An eighteen-year-old woman once asked me, "If you had to pick just *one* piece of advice that you felt would make a young person's life better than it already is, what would it be?"

If I had to choose, I'd suggest putting far more attention on being grateful. This one simple attitude, "the attitude of gratitude," has the power to change your life.

Being grateful means thinking more about what you have and what's right with your life than about what's wrong, what's missing, what needs to be better, and what you don't have.

This strategy sounds very simple, but the truth is, it's much easier said than done. Since we live in such an achievement-driven world, it's very easy to fall into the habit of focusing on what's lacking in your life, on the deficiencies and problems.

For example, if you get 95 percent of the answers correct on an exam, the first question often is, "What about the other five?" When I've won awards over the years, the first question I was asked has almost always been, "What's next?" In fact, if you see or hear me on a talk show discussing *this* book, I'll bet you the person doing the interview will ask, "What's the *next* book going to be?"

We all know how tempting it is to focus on the flaws of our body instead of what we like about it, or what's wrong with our parents, or our teachers, or our brain, or our skin, or whatever. If you do ten things in a day and nine of them go well, which one are you most likely to talk about during dinner? Almost always we choose to discuss the one thing that went wrong, the worst part of our day. It's almost like we've set ourselves up to be miserable. Our continual focus on what's missing, what's wrong, or how we need to be even better or get more done keeps us from being happy now.

As an experiment, try something new. Think more about what's *right* with your life than what's wrong. Start first thing in the morning by waking up and thinking about at least three things you have to be grateful for. If possible, write your answers down in a journal or on a sheet of paper. You'll be amazed at what will happen, how much happier you'll be, when you focus not on your imperfect skin, but on how lucky you are to have a functioning body; not on your mom's or dad's imperfections, but on how lucky you are to have someone who cares; not on what's wrong with you, but on something you like about yourself.

The other part of gratitude is the expression of gratitude to others. Just as you probably love it when someone tells you how much she appreciates you, others love to hear it too. Try, whenever possible, to remember not to take others for granted. Share your appreciation and gratitude. Say "thank you" and really mean it. Write thank-you notes when someone does something nice for you, or leave a nice message on his answering machine or voice mail, or send a thoughtful e-mail.

Expressing your appreciation will accomplish several things. First, it will heighten the joy of others—nothing means more to me than when one of my daughters (or someone else) lets me know that she isn't taking me for granted, that she appreciates me or something I'm doing. And, second, remembering to express your gratitude will direct your mind toward what's going well, what's right with your life, what's being done for you, and what you have to be grateful for. The nice thing is, when you're looking for what's right, you're going to find more of it.

Believe it or not, if you'll try expressing your gratitude, it will be a truly eye-opening experience. As you get used to doing it, you're going to notice a world of difference in the quality of your life.

# 70

# READ THE FINE PRINT

Monica was stressed out because a number of her friends weren't treating her the way she wanted to be treated. She told her counselor that she lived by the golden rule, which says, "Do unto others as you would have them do unto you." She couldn't understand what was going on. After all, she was treating others exactly the way she wanted to be treated.

Her counselor suggested something to her that made a world of difference. She asked Monica to consider the "fine print" in her golden rule. "What do you mean by fine print?" she asked. Her counselor explained that sometimes we make automatic assumptions about things that are important to us but we don't even know we're doing it because it seems so obvious that everyone would see it the same way. It's so hard for us to see these invisible assumptions that it's a lot like "fine print."

She suggested to Monica that if you were to include the fine print, her golden rule might actually go like this: "Do unto others as you would have them do unto you—and if you do, they will treat you well too." That last part would be nice, but it's not necessarily always true. Monica saw her attempts to be nice to others as a "contract," an automatic payback mechanism.

What Monica learned from her counselor was that treating people nicely is its own reward. If you think about it, it's true. When you're nice to people, you make them feel special. But what also happens is that your thoughtful intentions translate into happy, fulfilled feelings. In other words, when you wish people well in your mind, or when you do something nice for someone, or when you're thoughtful, kind, patient, considerate, forgiving, or generous, you are rewarded with similar feelings. It's been said that giving is its own reward. That's true, and it holds true for being nice as well.

Fine print shows up in many different ways. Athletes usually believe that winning is preferable to losing. That's perfectly understandable. The "fine print," however, might be, "If I lose, then I'm a loser." The same fine print can apply to students who don't get the grades they want, or to teens who can't have the boyfriend or girlfriend they desire. If you can identify and delete some of your own fine print, you can eliminate a great deal of your frustration.

# 71

# LOOK FOR THE INNOCENCE

How often do you feel misunderstood, or as if someone isn't giving you the benefit of the doubt? Most teens I've asked tell me it happens all the time. We do something and someone takes it wrong. Or we feel like someone is being too hard on us, or too judgmental. Sometimes we do something wrong or mean, but we didn't really mean it. Other times we're exhausted and don't respond in a friendly enough way or with enough gratitude or patience. Or we're in a really bad mood and we overreact to someone. Have you ever been in an enormous hurry, running really late, and cut in front of someone? Have you ever said to yourself, "That wasn't really me?" or, "I don't know what got into me?" Don't you wish that people would understand that, despite your occasional mistake or mess-up, you don't mean any harm? Don't you wish people would see you as you really are—innocent?

When you're dealing with people, whether you know them or not, it's often easier to see the guilt instead of the innocence. On the surface, people are doing all sorts of things that could either offend or irritate us. After all, people make mistakes, cut you off on the highway, use bad judgment, say the wrong thing, forget to express gratitude, blow smoke in your face, spill things, fail to apologize, make too much noise, act weird, and dozens of other things. Everywhere you look, people are being all too human!

Seeing the innocence in people is a very freeing experience. It helps to transform you from a person who is irritated, frustrated, or bothered by others to a person who is rarely stressed out. It really helps you to stop sweating the small stuff!

Seeing the innocence doesn't mean you excuse all negative behavior or allow people to take advantage of you. Rather, it means you cut people some slack and allow them to be human. It involves acknowledging the fact that, like you, a vast majority of the time people aren't out to ruin your day or frustrate you. Instead, they are doing the best they can to make it through their own day. They might be having a tough day, or be in an enormous hurry, or in a horrible mood, or be dealing with a crisis. Who knows? As in your case—and in mine—there is usually a good reason why people are acting the way they are.

Looking for the innocence in the behavior of others is a huge relief. Instead of reacting so harshly or abruptly to events, you'll be able to keep things in their proper perspective, maintain a sense of humor, and not allow so many things to adversely affect your day.

# 72

# DON'T EXAGGERATE
# YOUR TROUBLES

This is a hard strategy to write about because all of us—including me—believe that our troubles are significant. If we didn't, they wouldn't bother us so much.

I've noticed, however, that many people tend to exaggerate their troubles and the hassles they must deal with. The problem with doing so is that it encourages you to sweat the small stuff and to imagine that your life is even harder than it actually is. This prophecy becomes self-fulfilling, encouraging you to focus on the difficult and negative aspects of your life.

The tendency to exaggerate your troubles comes out in many ways. People will say things like, "I work fourteen hours a day," or, "I have five hours a night of homework." The truth might be more like ten hours a day or three hours of homework. Still a lot of work, but not quite as bad as someone can make it out to be. The problem here is that if you convince yourself you work even more hours than you actually do, you'll start to believe you have no time and that you're exhausted. Your imagined frustration will feed on itself, and you'll become more irritable and less patient, thus causing you to become even more stressed out.

Thirteen-year-old Stephen claimed that he had "no friends" and that "everyone at school hated him." That was the exaggerated version of the truth. The actual truth was that he only had a few friends and that he wanted more. Further, he had been teased at school by a few bullies and had interpreted that to mean that "everyone hated him." In truth, the bullies were selfish and self-centered jerks who teased anyone who couldn't defend themselves against them.

I certainly wouldn't deny that Stephen was having a hard time. Yet his gross exaggeration of his problems made it seem to him that his life was falling apart. It wasn't. He simply needed to keep his problems in perspective and try to find more like-minded friends.

It's hard to admit to yourself that you might be exaggerating your troubles. Yet if it's true that you are doing so, and if you can face the truth, you'll be rewarded with less stress and a happier life.

# 73

# DEVELOP A THEME
# FOR THE DAY

A number of years ago I experimented with this strategy and found that whenever I would do it, I would inevitably have a pretty good day. What's more, it's really easy and it only takes a few seconds.

The idea here is to spend a few moments each morning deciding on a theme for the day. The simple act of declaring the goal seems to plant a mental seed and have the suggestive power to make it happen, at least to some degree. If you try it, I think you'll be quite surprised at the results. What seems to happen is that you will notice yourself being more patient (or whatever other theme you have going). You'll also notice those times when you're not being so patient. Having a theme brings the issue to your consciousness.

For example, the last time I had "patience" as my theme for the day, the telephone repair person was over an hour late, and I was getting really bothered. Then, all of a sudden, I caught myself and remembered my theme. The result was that instead of getting too uptight and stressed, I was able to nip my emotions in the bud. I calmly called the phone company and asked them to hurry up. The person on the phone sensed that I wasn't being too demanding or unreasonable and was able to get someone out to help me fairly quickly.

Other possible themes might include kindness, compassion, thoughtfulness, listening, humor, eye contact, forgiveness, friendliness, understanding, optimism, concentration, perspective, and lightheartedness. You can choose anything that you feel might make your day a little better. Try each of these and many others. See which ones make a difference. You can get on a rotation or simply make them up as you go.

Sixteen-year-old Maraca decided to have a one-day theme of gratitude. He said it was the strangest thing. The simple act of deciding to make gratitude a part of his day made his day among the best he had ever had. He said he noticed more things about his life to be grateful for than at any other time. He even thanked a girl for coming to his rescue in class when he was asked a question. He'd never realized that simply being appreciative to someone could lead to a nice discussion over lunch and a possible new girlfriend. Who knows what gifts may present themselves?

# 74

# APPLY THE 1–10 SCALE

I love this strategy and try to remember to apply it every time I feel myself getting too uptight or stressed out. It's certainly not scientific, but it seems to work pretty well. It's based on the assumption that not all, but many, of the things we treat as a really big deal aren't quite as important as we make them out to be. This is a simple way to stop sweating the small stuff!

Since I travel a great deal, I've learned a few packing tricks, especially pertaining to my tendency to overpack. Essentially, the key is to pack as little as you think you can possibly get away with. Then close your suitcase and walk away. A little while later, open the suitcase and remove exactly half of all that remains. I'm not exaggerating—half. I've found that if I do this, I usually still have more than I need on my trips. Most times we think we're going to need far more than we actually do.

The 1–10 scale works with a similar perspective. The idea is that not always, but often, things aren't as bad as we initially think they are. And if we remind ourselves of this, especially when we're starting to get stressed out, often we can put things back into their relative scale of importance.

The 1–10 scale has to do with the relative significance you give to something that is bothering you. Suppose, for example, you're annoyed that a friend forgot to do something she had promised. You feel a little hurt and bothered, and start to think about the other times she's done the same thing. You feel yourself getting uptight.

*Now* is the time to apply the first phase of the 1–10 scale. Think about the issue and apply a number between one and ten, indicating how important you think it is. One would be very unimportant and ten would be monumental. For argument's sake, suppose you choose #4. Now, for a few minutes, try to forget about it. Walk away and do something else.

Awhile later, think about the issue again and the number you applied to its importance. Now, just as you do with determining how much to pack in your suitcase, cut the number in half. In my experience, not all but most of the time you're going to be right on the mark in terms of its actual importance. So, in our example here, you would apply a value of two to your friend messing up. And if something is a #2, it's not worth losing any sleep over—or sweating!

After a while, this will become second nature. You'll cut your initial assumption in half virtually without even thinking about it. More important, you'll begin to believe that the lesser of the two assumptions is usually the correct one. What seems to happen is that you start to assume that blowing things out of proportion is a natural human tendency, and you begin to factor that assumption into your everyday reactions. As a result, you'll become a little suspicious of your initial (over)reactions. So, rather than becoming so upset about things and remaining upset, you'll start to assume that whatever it is you're so upset about probably isn't quite as bad as you're making it out to be. Congratulations! You're learning to stop sweating the small stuff.

# 75

# REMAIN OPTIMISTIC

If you look carefully at the people who tend to sweat the small stuff the most, you'll find that most of them are, to one degree or another, pessimists. They are either convinced or at least expecting that things will turn out badly. They're looking for "what's wrong." They are a little skeptical and cynical. When things do go wrong, they'll say, "See, what did I tell you?"

If you think about it, the characteristics of a pessimist are very consistent with someone who would sweat the small stuff: picky, negative, easily upset and bothered by things, frustrated that life isn't perfect, and often critical of people who are trying to do good in the world. Pessimists spend a good deal of energy complaining that life isn't meeting their expectations.

Interestingly enough, pessimists usually don't call themselves that. Instead, they will refer to themselves as "realists." They will insist that the only reason they expect things to go wrong is that so much does go wrong in the world. They usually are very good at validating their beliefs with concrete evidence. Therefore, they will almost always call an optimist "unrealistic."

It's fascinating, however, to consider that optimists and pessimists live in the same world. So, the question becomes: "Who is right?" The answer, of course, is that both are right. It all depends on what you choose to focus on. You can focus on what's right with the world: the good, the beauty, kindness, compassion, and thoughtfulness. You can notice the wonders of nature and the beauty around you. You can marvel at success, possibilities, miracles, and the gift of life itself. You can look at all that's right.

Or you can focus on what's wrong with the world: the ugliness and cruelty. You can complain about the jerks in the world, and, when you look at nature, you can see the litter and graffiti that exists. It's all up to you.

Becoming more optimistic is a choice, plain and simple. You merely have to see what's in it for you: happiness, less stress, better relationships, more gratitude, and more fun. The rest will take care of itself.

Don't be concerned that being or becoming an optimist will make you unrealistic. That's just a myth. Optimists acknowledge that there is plenty of pain and suffering in the world and that there are endless problems to overcome and deal with. In fact, because optimists are less bogged down by the negative events and conditions of the world, they end up doing more than pessimists to solve those problems. Rather than giving up or remaining hopeless, they know that their small acts of love make a big difference to the world they live in. So, remain optimistic. You'll not only be sweating the small stuff less often in your life, but you'll be making an important contribution as well.

# 76

# EMPATHIZE

Learning to empathize is a great way to become not only a more gracious and thoughtful person, but a happier one as well. To empathize means that you attempt to put yourself in others' shoes, to experience something from their perspective. It doesn't mean you feel sorry for them, but that you seek to understand what it must feel like to be them—or what it must be like to be going through what they are going through.

Imagine, for a moment, that there is a new kid at school. He's awkward and lonely. He has no friends, no one to talk to. He's shy and frightened. To empathize with this person would mean you would imagine what it must be like to be him right now. You might think, "Gee, that would be tough," or something like that. Your empathetic feelings probably would translate into some type of thoughtful behavior. You might go out of your way to say hello, for example, or you might suggest that others do the same. At very least, you'd be absolutely sure to be sensitive to the fact that what he's going through is difficult, so you wouldn't even think of being insensitive or mean-spirited.

The opposite of empathy would be indifference, the feeling of, "So what, it's not me so why should I care?" This more selfish way of thinking about things tends to translate into equally selfish ways of acting. An indifferent person would never go out of his or her way to be welcoming or inclusive. In fact, it's possible such a person might even go out of his or her way to be cruel.

Empathy, then, is characterized by a sense of caring and interest in others, while indifference is made up of self-centeredness and apathy.

It's fairly obvious why developing one's empathy increases one's character and warmth as a human being. It means you take some of your attention off yourself and put it on others. Doing so makes you a nicer person, easier to be around and more compassionate.

What's not so obvious, however, is that developing your empathy also serves to heighten your own level of happiness and to greatly reduce your stress.

Empathetic people care about others and their feelings, so they feel connected with others rather than isolated. This connection keeps them from feeling threatened when other people are successful, good-looking, or talented. Instead, they are able to share in the joy that other people experience. People are drawn toward empathetic people; they want to spend time with them, help them, listen to them.

Empathetic people are acutely aware of the fact that we're all human. Therefore, it's easy for them to be forgiving when people make mistakes or mess up. And they extend this perspective to themselves as well. Rather than beat themselves up or act overly self-critical, they instead learn from their mistakes and move on.

There's a real upside to becoming more empathetic, but no downside whatsoever. What's more, empathy is easy to develop. All it takes is the willingness to put yourself in the shoes of others. Take the step today. The benefits will last a lifetime.

# 77

# LOOK WHO'S DOING YOGA

Awhile back I picked up a copy of *Yoga Journal* magazine and, there on the cover, was singing sensation Sting. I've since learned that many famous entertainers, sports stars, and other notable and interesting people practice yoga on a regular basis. In fact, I'd be surprised if at least a few of your favorite stars aren't practicing yoga. And why not? Yoga has the potential to help you create a more peaceful body, mind, and spirit. What's more, it's simple, relaxing, easy to learn, and fun. It's also very popular.

I've been doing yoga for about twenty years. I started because of some back pain and stiffness I was having in college. I was renting a room in someone's home, and my landlord gave me a book called *Richard Hittleman's Yoga: 28 Day Exercise Plan*. I was hooked right away. Today I still practice yoga, not only for the physical benefits, but also for the peace of mind and sense of calm it delivers to my mind and spirit. Almost always, when I finish my fifteen-minute routine, I'm left feeling happy and peaceful. After a few minutes of yoga, it's almost hard to imagine sweating the small stuff. You simply feel too calm and centered to allow yourself to be rattled. The people around you will notice the changes in you too. They will sense a deeper presence in your eyes and in your way of being. You'll be more peaceful and relaxed.

Essentially, yoga is a series of poses and stretches that energize your body, leaving you feeling calm, balanced, and focused. While I'm far from being an expert, one of my best friends, Mark, is a phenomenal instructor. He assures me that the benefits I feel from yoga are also experienced by almost everyone who practices on a regular basis. Mark is one of the most peaceful people I've ever known.

I'm super glad that I took up yoga at a young age, and I encourage you to do the same. I'm positive that it will be an activity that I continue to practice and explore for the rest of my life. The rewards are immense, and yoga seems to be appropriate for people of virtually any age or level of fitness. If you'd like to learn more, you can pick up any number of good books at your local bookstore or library, or, if possible, you can look into taking a yoga class. There are also great videotapes available that can teach you how to do it. You can find them advertised in yoga or health magazines.

Yoga is one of those activities that, prior to trying it, you probably can't even imagine doing it. In fact, you might be rolling your eyes. Yet once you've tried it a few times, you can't imagine not doing it. It's that relaxing. The motivation to try yoga is the promise of a more peaceful way of being. So, give it a try. Be adventurous. It just may be an activity that you'll love for the rest of your life.

## 78

# BE CAREFUL THAT YOU'RE NOT PRACTICING BEING UNHAPPY

"What do you mean? I'd never do that!" These are the types of responses I usually get from teens when I make this type of suggestion. And that's a natural reaction. Of course you wouldn't "practice" being unhappy—at least not intentionally. After all, no one would harm his own spirit, at least on purpose.

One thing you've undoubtedly learned already in our achieve, achieve, "more is better" world is that the way to get really good at something is to practice it. So, it follows that if you were practicing being unhappy, eventually you'd become an expert. But what do I mean by "practicing being unhappy"?

Suppose, for argument's sake, that your goal was to be as unhappy, frustrated, and stressed out as possible. What would you need to do? The only way to guarantee that you would succeed would be to think lots of unhappy, angry, stressful thoughts. Without them, you wouldn't be able to be as unhappy as you'd like. Because our thoughts are so closely linked to our state of mind and the way we feel, we need to think negatively before we actually can feel that way. If you don't believe me, give it a try. Just try to get upset right now without first thinking about something that upsets you.

We're always thinking, every moment of the day. It's just that we're not always *aware* that we're doing so. Let me explain:

Thinking is a little like breathing in the sense that, until you read the word "breathing" just now, you probably weren't aware of your breath. Thinking is like that too. It goes on and on, whether we're aware of it or not. The problem is, if we're not aware of the link and connection between our thoughts and the way we feel, our thoughts can—and often do—encourage us to feel bad. This, in turn, can encourage us to act out in negative ways.

Some of our thoughts are happy, positive, compassionate, hopeful, productive, loving, strategic, helpful, or kind. Others, however, are negative, pessimistic, self-defeating, worrisome, angry, hateful, jealous, or harmful. I'm not suggesting that all your thoughts need to be positive or that there's anything wrong with having negative thoughts. But you probably can see that unless you're aware that you're thinking negatively, and that your thoughts are at least partially responsible for the way you're feeling, then, in effect, you *are* practicing being unhappy—without even knowing it. Remember, you're still having the thoughts.

Here's something to try: The next time you feel angry, sad, frustrated, stressed out, or otherwise negative, remember this strategy. Check in with the thoughts you're having. Chances are, they are going to be right in line with how you're feeling. In other words, if you're sad, you're probably having sad thoughts.

If you can catch yourself thinking negatively and drop those thoughts, then very often you can snap yourself out of a negative state of mind simply by realizing, "Oh, it's just my thoughts again." To this day, I catch myself having "thought attacks" all the time in my car, the shower, on airplanes and elsewehere. I'll be mentally rehearsing some upcoming event and thinking about how bad it's going to be when, all of a sudden, it's as if I wake up and say to myself, "Wow, there I go again. My thoughts are making me worried."

Once you see that your thoughts are just thoughts and that they can't hurt you without your own consent, it will be like a game to you. You'll be able to drop your thoughts, dismiss them, ignore them, or change them—not all the time, but at least far more often.

This doesn't mean that it's always going to be easy, but it sure helps get you back on track. I think you'll be amazed at the results.

# 79

# CUT YOUR LOSSES

This has to be one of the most practical strategies in the book. Everyone makes mistakes, says the wrong thing, and goofs up. That's just part of being human. A great deal of stress, however, stems not so much from our mistakes but rather from what we either do or don't do after making a mistake.

In some ways, it gets down to how graceful and humble we can be. For example, if you "blow it"—get caught cheating, lying, talking behind someone else's back, damaging someone else's property, being insensitive, hurting someone's feelings, or whatever—and you can admit to what you've done and offer a sincere apology, willingly and gracefully, then most of the time you'll probably be OK. Your "damage control" will be done.

As long as it's clear that you've learned from your mistake, and you're sincere in your remorse, most people will give you another chance. You'll feel some stress, but it will be minimized. With any luck, whatever happened will be put behind you and laid to rest. And if, by chance, you're not forgiven, at least you can know that you've done your best to make amends and rectify the situation. You can live with yourself and go on.

If, on the other hand, you compound the problem by making excuses, blaming others, becoming defensive, and running away, you will have created tons of additional stress for yourself, guaranteed. Whoever was hurt or affected by your mistake will assume you'll do it again. You won't be trusted or given another chance. Your reputation will be damaged. People will talk behind your back. Further, your conscience will be affected because you will not have given the other party a chance to forgive your actions. Whatever you've done will be there, somewhere in the back of your mind.

One day, when Mike was a teen, he was joking around with some friends. He made an insensitive, disgusting, racist comment. He didn't know it, but he was being watched by a person of that particular race. When he turned around and saw the person, his heart sank, and he felt like an idiot, a complete jerk. He couldn't believe what he had done.

Mike was at a crossroads. His friends were standing right there. The person he had insulted was too.

He made one of the best decisions of his life. In a humble and sincere tone, he asked the person if he would allow him to apologize. Luckily for him, the person he had just insulted allowed him to continue.

Mike offered his most gracious apology and admitted that what he had done was inexcusable and pathetic. He said that he had just been trying to be "cool" and that he didn't mean what he said. His apology was accepted by the person because of his sincerity.

Had he gone the other way and continued to act like a jerk, or had he run away, or laughed, there's no telling what would have happened. He may have caused a fight and certainly he would have deeply hurt another human being's feelings. What's more, he would have had to live with himself and his ugliness for the rest of his life, knowing he didn't have the guts to apologize.

What Mike did was wrong. Yet even something this bad was helped by his ability to "cut his losses." When I first heard Mike's story, it really hit me. To this day, I always do my best to cut my own losses. I hope you will too.

# 80

# EXAMINE YOUR HEADLINES

Just as a newspaper always has a series of headline stories designed to grab your attention, so do the rest of us in our personal lives. Our personal headlines are the stories that we highlight in our minds and share with others. They are the stories and personality traits we tend to emphasize and focus on, the ones we give the most attention to. Sometimes our headlines are reoccurring; other times they are somewhat isolated.

The reason it's so important to examine our headlines is that often we don't even realize what they are. Our headlines become so automatic that we don't even see them. Yet even though we don't see them, they affect our lives in significant ways. Many times we define ourselves as a certain type of person without even knowing it. That's important to realize because maybe we don't want to define ourselves that way.

I'll give you a personal example. Years ago I got into the habit of being too busy. I would schedule too many things and then complain that I never had any time. I would remind myself over and over again how extremely busy I was. When people would ask me how I was, I'd usually slip into the conversation that I was "really busy." Without knowing it, my "busyness" had become my personal headline, my own little harmless drama. People would think of me as "busy" and would try to accommodate me by not taking too much of my time.

At some point, as an experiment, I decided to examine my headlines and discovered that busyness was my lead story. All of a sudden, I realized how silly it was—I was defining myself as busy. It seemed to me that my life was bigger than that, and I didn't want to limit myself by that narrow definition.

The simple act of recognizing what I had done enabled me to back off. I learned to dismiss my thoughts of being too busy; I cut back my schedule a little bit and tried hard not to overemphasize my busyness to others. As a result, I felt calmer and less pressured. It seemed as if I had more time. I wasn't in such a constant hurry. The people in my life noticed the change right away. They would say things like, "You seem more peaceful," and ask: "What's different?" It was easy to make a slight change. It all started by examining my headlines.

I've talked to teens who have found this exercise to be eye-opening and helpful. Some recognized that being "overly dramatic" had become their predominant headline. Others realized that, when talking to others, they were virtually always "bothered" by something. Still others said that they were "Usually mad at someone." One young woman said that she had learned to define herself as a "troublemaker." In these examples and so many others, you can see that being aware of your own tendencies and of the ways you define yourself can be very useful if, in fact, you want to make a change.

While it's important to examine your headlines, it's also important to know that headlines aren't necessarily bad. Often they are wonderful. The idea isn't to be self-critical, but self-observant. Check in with yourself and you might decide to make a change—or you might not. It's up to you, but at least you'll have the information at your fingertips. I've found that knowing what you're working with is usually an advantage.

# 81

# NOTICE YOUR PARENTS
# DOING THINGS RIGHT

One of the most consistent complaints I've heard over the years from teens about their parents is that parents have a strong tendency to notice what their teens are doing wrong, but usually fail to see all the things they are doing right. Many teens have told me, "If my parents would only notice more of what I do right and how hard I'm trying, it would be much easier for me to be motivated to do even better, and it would be a ton easier to be around them."

I've been a teen, and I've been a parent. My experience as a teen was that teens are absolutely right in their assessment—parents *do* tend to notice the negative far more than the positive. And I agree, this is counterproductive to motivation, self-esteem, communication, and positive feelings. If parents, including me, could remember this obvious law of life, we would get along even better with our kids, and they would appreciate us much more than they do.

Ironically, however, my experience as a parent is exactly the same as my experience was as a teen. My kids—and *all* of my friends' kids—tend to do the very same thing: They notice what we parents are doing wrong more than they notice what we do that is right. Yet people are people, whether we are sixteen years old or forty-six. We're motivated more by positive reinforcement than we are by negative. We respond better to praise than we do to criticism, and we tend to live up (or down) to the expectations of others, especially family members.

One parent I met has five children, including a fourteen-year-old son. In addition to all the normal stuff she does with him and his brothers and sisters, four times a week she takes him to his year-round athletic practice. She pays for the sport, makes sure he has all the necessary gear, packs his daily snack, takes him to the doctor when he's injured, attends virtually all the games, supports him in every way she knows how, and even takes his teammates to and from practice on a regular basis. Needless to say, she sacrifices a great deal for her son, and, as is often the case, the best she gets is an occasional "thanks for the ride."

Not too long ago, she was running behind and got him to practice a little late, for the first time in more than a year. You would have thought the world was coming to an end! He laid into her, furious that she had made this mistake. She, of course, was upset with his overreaction, and the two ended up mad at one another for the rest of the evening.

My take on this event was that he made her feel the same way you might feel when you work hard on something and all your parents notice is what you did wrong, or the mistakes you made, or how you "could have done better." Their disappointment overshadows their pride in your work and effort, and it hurts. It probably also makes you angry.

As an experiment, see if you can begin to notice all the things your parents do right—how many times they get you where you need to be on time, how often a meal is made for you, or a form is filled out, or something you've lost is found, or you're allowed to do something, or something is paid for.

I can assure you that I make the same suggestion to parents, so believe me, I'm not taking sides. I also can assure you that, if you can notice more of what they do right instead of what they do wrong—or how you wish they were different—the stress you experience will lessen and your day-to-day experience of life will improve. You'll feel better because the blessings in your life will become more obvious, and your attention will be focused on positive rather than negative energy. Your parents will be easier to deal with too because they will feel more appreciated and valued. Who knows? Maybe your good example will rub off on them and they will begin to notice more of what you're doing right too.

# 82

# BECOME A LITTLE
# LESS STUBBORN

Eric's mother told me that her son was so stubborn she didn't know what to do. When I asked fifteen-year-old Eric what he thought, he yelled out, "I am not stubborn!" If you would have asked me the same question when I was fifteen, I probably would have said the same thing, in the same tone of voice.

Such is the nature of stubbornness. It's easy for others to see, but really difficult to detect in ourselves. One of the problems with being stubborn is that, when you are, you'll probably be sweating the small stuff—a lot. Things will get to you easily because of your tense mind-set. After all, being stubborn means you don't want to listen to others, so you close your mind. Doing so, in turn, makes you want to prove your position at any cost. You dig in your heels and refuse to budge.

Another problem with being stubborn is that, much of the time, you'll insist on being right. You have to think about, focus on, and even point out when others are wrong. The problem here is that doing so creates irritation and frustration inside of you, making you even more tense. This encourages even more things to bother you, and on and on.

It's much easier said than done, but the way to become a little less stubborn is to learn to say the words, "You're right," and really mean it. Ouch! I know this can be difficult. And what makes it even more difficult is that, if you want to become less stressed and stubborn, you're going to have to bite your lip and learn to say these words (depending on the situation) to your parents, your teachers, your boss, your neighbors, and even your friends and siblings.

The words, "You're right," speak to the heart of the matter. They defuse your stubbornness. It's a statement of humility; the acknowledgment that you are willing to listen, soften, learn, and admit that, at least some of the time, others know things that you don't. You can admit that, like the rest of us, you not only make mistakes, but you can learn from them as well.

Seventeen-year-old John was arrested and put into juvenile hall for beating up and injuring a classmate. He was so stubborn that, even after he was told that a genuine apology would probably help his chances of getting out, he refused. He insisted that his violence was justified. Even in reading about John, can't you feel the stress of the stubbornness? Can't you also feel how emotionally freeing it would be for him simply to admit that he had made a mistake—that he was wrong?

Whether it involves something really serious, as in John's case, or something far more ordinary—having to win a silly argument or refusing to admit you made a mistake or that you lost something—being stubborn is highly stressful. The good news is, the reverse is equally true. Letting go of your need to be stubborn is extremely freeing. You'll feel better right away. And, what's more, you'll probably be rewarded with positive reinforcement from everyone around you. Everyone loves people who are humble enough to admit when they are wrong and who are willing to learn. Becoming a little less stubborn goes a long, long way. Give it a try, and you'll see what I mean.

# 83

# REMEMBER TO BE KIND

I once asked a group of teens, "What is the most rewarding part of life?" The initial answers were things like being popular, being cool, having a boyfriend/girlfriend, fitting in, having fun, succeeding at something, winning, and looking good. Then a young woman at the back of room stood up and said, "To be honest, the most rewarding part of my life is when I remember to be kind." She went on to tell two stories. The first was about a time when she had befriended a new student at school, and the second was when she was with her grandmother, holding her hand, as her grandmother died.

From the moment she told her stories, the emotions in the room went through some sort of almost magical transformation. It was as if everyone began to reexamine what the word "rewarding" really meant to them. The same people who, five minutes earlier, had said that "being popular" was the most rewarding part of their life, asked if they could share something different, something having to do with kindness. All the teens were able to remember a time when they were really kind to someone, and they all agreed that it had made them feel really good.

If you think about the times you've been extra kind to someone— very thoughtful, generous, respectful, or just plain old nice—you'll probably be able to see the link between simple acts of kindness and a feeling of genuine satisfaction. In fact, chances are, many of your fondest memories will involve an act of kindness, either by you or by someone else.

This topic is a very important one to spend some time thinking about because most of us spend a huge percentage of our time, all throughout our lives, chasing things that we believe are going to make us happy—success, the ideal boyfriend or girlfriend, good looks, achievements—when in fact the one thing that brings us continual, guaranteed, ongoing satisfaction is old-fashioned kindness. And what's more, being kind is simple, natural, effortless, and free.

It's difficult to sweat the small stuff very often when you're tuned into kindness because your mind is geared in such a positive direction. You'll be easier on yourself, more patient, easier to get along with, and more optimistic. In addition, you'll give people a break when they are less than perfect, and you'll take yourself a little less seriously.

So whether you do nice things for people, act courteous, are compassionate, are polite, are grateful, or, I hope, all of the above, think kindness. Everyone around you will benefit, and the greatest reward will be yours.

# 84

# TAKE CRITICISM
# A LITTLE LESS PERSONALLY

I've received a number of letters and e-mails from teens indicating that one of the hardest things about being a teen is dealing with criticism from others. I have found that there is a way to deflect not all, but most, of the sting of criticism. It has to do with taking criticism a little less personally.

For just a moment, I'd like to you to forget everything you think about criticism—how much it occurs, how much you resent it, whether it's justified, and why it exists. Let's take a step back and see what criticism really is.

We can only say a few things for certain about the nature of criticism. First, it reflects someone else's opinion. That opinion may have a grain of truth in it, or it may be utter nonsense. If it's nonsense, we don't have to worry too much about it. For example, if someone said to you, "I hate the way you tie your shoes. I think you should you wrap them in cellophane instead," you'd probably roll your eyes and dismiss the comment. You wouldn't take it personally.

On the other hand, if there is a grain of truth in the criticism, we are wise to try to learn from it. A few years ago, for example, someone raised a hand after one of my lectures and, in front of more than a hundred people, said, "I think you talk too fast. It really bugs me." As I thought about it later on, I realized that, despite his abrupt delivery, he had made a pretty good point. I do have a tendency to speak too quickly. Since that time I've learned to slow down and have become a better speaker as a result.

Beyond the degree of accuracy—the right and wrong of it all—there is one thing that is always true about criticism. When someone criticizes you, it may or may not say very much about the real you—it may or may not be entirely accurate—but it always speaks to that person's need to be critical. In other words, if I attack you with criticism, I am telling you that I, Richard, am a person who has the need to be critical. That need may come from my desire to be listened to or heard, or it may stem from a bad mood or pure frustration. It could also, of course, be coming from a genuine desire to be of help. But regardless of my motivation, the fact that I'm being critical of you means I have the need to be critical. This fact doesn't mean that I'm bad or wrong, only that I have this need.

When you put criticism into this perspective, it's easy to see that criticism has more to do with the person doing the criticizing than it does about you. That's why I didn't have to take the man's criticism personally in front of all those people. He was expressing his need to be critical. That's okay; we all seem to have that need every once in a while. I certainly do. While it turned out that I learned a great deal from his comments, I don't think I would have had I become defensive and taken it personally.

I'm not advocating that you tune out suggestions. In fact, the result will be just the opposite. When you don't take suggestions and criticism personally, you'll be more open to what is being said, and your learning curve will sharpen. You'll see it less as a threat or as an attack and more as a need that people have. Can you imagine how much happier we'd all be and how much less we'd be "sweating" if we didn't take criticism personally?

The next time you feel attacked by criticism, see if you can apply this strategy. Rather than taking the criticism personally, turn it around. Realize that the criticism is saying more about the person doing the criticizing than it says about you. You might find that it doesn't hurt so much.

# 85

# UNDERSTAND THE
# FOUR PILLARS OF THOUGHT:
# PILLAR #1—THE WHAT

Since thinking is perhaps the most powerful tool you have at your disposal to improve the quality of your life instantly, it will be important and helpful to you if you can gain an understanding of what I like to call the four pillars of thought. If you were to master each of the four pillars, you'd probably find that your life would become a whole lot easier and less complicated. You'd certainly feel less stressed, and would get along with others a little better. For that reason, I'm going to dedicate this and the next three strategies to these four topics.

Pillar #1 has to do with what you think about. Obviously, if you were to think nothing but angry, frustrated thoughts, twenty-four hours a day, your life would consist of mostly angry and frustrated feelings—a pretty dark existence. It would be difficult, if not impossible, to experience joy or laughter, or for you to be nice to anyone else. Luckily, most of us don't think exclusively negative thoughts or anything close to it. Yet it's also true that most of us probably have never spent much time or energy reflecting on what the nature of the majority of our thoughts are like either. In other words, do you know what percentage of your thoughts are happy, insecure, angry, stressed, jealous, productive, and fearful?

Imagine that you were trying to make some old-fashioned, home-made vegetable soup. You'd probably look for the freshest carrots, celery, tomatoes, mushrooms, onions, and peas. As important, you'd avoid all spoiled or rotten foods, and wouldn't even consider adding a single ingredient that would ruin your end result. The reason: You would know, with absolute certainty, that if you were to deviate from quality ingredients, your soup would surely suffer. Likewise, you would be aware that by sticking to a proven recipe, success is almost guaranteed.

In a way, what you think about is one of the most important ingredients of your life. To a large degree, the thoughts you add to the mix determine the feelings you experience and the behavior you put into action.

This is very simple but powerful. Once you equate what you think about directly with the quality of your life, you'll find yourself paying closer attention to the thoughts you allow to enter your mind. And when negative or hurtful thoughts do occur, you'll find yourself dismissing them much more quickly or attaching less significance to them. A high school student, Jason, told me that this "soup metaphor" was more helpful to him than any other he had ever heard. He told me, "I've become very selective, almost selfish, about what thoughts make the cut. I think in negative terms only when it's truly necessary." By making this one small change in his life, he told me his life was "about a hundred times better in every sense of the word."

Why put negative, hateful, self-defeating, angry, or frustrated thoughts into the mix when you know, with absolute certainty, that the result will be spoiled feelings? You'll discover that, the more you ask this question, the more picky you'll become. Let's go on to pillar #2.

# 86

# PILLAR #2—THE WHEN

Pillar #2 has to do with *when* you think about something, which is often as important, if not more important, than *what* you think about.

We've already discussed the subject of moods. We found out that, if your mood is right, you can think about (or discuss) virtually anything—problems, fears, issues, disagreements, plans, whatever. Given the right state of mind, you'll be adequately equipped with the necessary insights, calmness, perspective, and wisdom to enable to you solve problems, see solutions, figure things out, and get through practically anything.

On the other hand, if your mood is low enough, what's the point? You'll blow things out of proportion, things will seem worse than they actually are, and you'll be negative, pessimistic, and defensive.

In other words, it's all in the timing.

Imagine for a moment that you are in a terrible mood, feeling angry, resentful, and defensive. Further, your mother (or a friend, or someone you're in a relationship with, or an instructor, or a sibling, or someone you're in conflict with) is in a similar mood. Now imagine that there is something truly significant that you must discuss with your mom (or other person). When should you do it? Should you have your talk when you're both in a bad frame of mind—or even when you alone are in a bad state of mind? The answer, of course, is, "Not unless you absolutely have to." And even then, you'd still be better off at least being aware of the "mood factor" so that you could immunize yourself against crazy thinking!

So, the question isn't whether we must think about painful or difficult things at least some of the time—we do—but, rather, when is the optimal and wisest time to do so? Again, the answer is to try to think about difficult subjects when you're most equipped to do so: when you're feeling secure, when your mood is up.

The hard part is that when your mood is up, you may not be motivated to think about difficult things because you won't feel the urgency that you do when your mood is lower. But it's when your mood is down that you will feel compelled to think about all the problems and issues in your life. Again, that's not the time to do so because you will be lacking the necessary wisdom, perspective, and compassion that is required to sort things out. Let's move on to pillar #3.

# 87

# PILLAR #3—THE HOW

People spend time thinking in essentially two different and distinct ways. Both are extremely important and easily recognizable. Pillar #3 has to do with *how* you think—beginning to recognize which type of thinking you are engaged in. And then, occasionally, shifting from one type of thought to the other.

The first way that you think is a little like a computer. It's very analytical. This is the way you think when you are learning something new or when you are trying to figure things out. When you use this type of thinking, usually at least some effort is involved. When we call on this type of thinking, we fill our minds with data, call on memories, and actively pursue our thoughts. We work at it.

The other way we use our mind is when we think without effort. This type of thinking sometimes doesn't even feel like thinking because it happens all by itself when your mind is clear. It's a natural process that occurs when you aren't trying to think. You might call it "soft" thinking.

When we use this soft type of thinking, ideas come to us, almost as if out of the blue. We relax and it seems that our thinking is done for us, almost automatically. But this type of thinking can be extremely wise and practical. For example, you've probably had the experience of trying really hard to remember someone's name and couldn't do it. So, you gave up and went on to something else. Then, out of the blue, the person's name popped into your mind. Or you may have been unable to figure out a solution to a problem, such as how to solve a conflict with someone. All of a sudden, while in the shower or while walking to school, the answer appears. That's what I'm talking about. These are examples of soft thinking.

It's important to know the difference between the two ways of thinking (to recognize how you are thinking) because when you're sweating the small stuff or when you're frustrated about something or unable to come up with an answer, quite often you're trying too hard. Or, put another way, you're thinking—but maybe too much in the effort mode and not enough in the softer mode.

As an experiment, see what happens to your frustration when, instead of rolling up your sleeves and thinking even harder about certain problems, you take a few deep breaths and call upon your reflective thinking instead. The hard part is that you have to trust that, even though it won't seem as if you're doing as much, you are still, very much, taking charge of your problems. You're just doing it in a slightly different, softer way.

It's not that one type of thinking is good and the other is bad. Both types play an important role in your life. The problem, as I see it, is that most of us seem to rely too much on our analytical thinking, especially when it isn't working. You don't have to be frustrated or stressed out to use the softer type of thinking. In fact, you can use it whenever the analytical thinking isn't necessary. Experiment; you may be pleasantly surprised at how easily certain issues will begin to resolve themselves and how much less often you blow things out of proportion. Let's move on to the fourth and final pillar of thought.

# 88

# PILLAR #4—THE FACT OF

I know it sounds obvious, but you and I are thinking creatures. Believe it or not, however, it's easy to forget that we are thinking because it's so automatic. It's sort of like breathing. Until this second, when I brought it up, you had probably not thought too much about breathing either, because it happens automatically too.

I hope by now that you are totally convinced that your thinking plays a significant role in the quality of your life. Pillar #4 has to do with the very fact that we are thinking, and that our thinking is affecting our entire experience of life.

Recognizing my own thinking is like waking up to the fact that I'm thinking. For example, say I start to feel overwhelmed about my schedule; I'll be thinking about how busy I am and how little time I have and so on. I'll convince myself that I'm busier than everyone else, and I'll be conjuring up all sorts of reasons why it happens. I'll even start to feel sorry for myself.

Then, all of a sudden, I'll wake up and recognize that my mind is filled up with my to-do list. I've been having a "thought attack" without even knowing I was doing so! This recognition instantly makes me feel better because, all of a sudden, I'm reminded that my sense of being overwhelmed is being created not from my life but from the fact that I'm obsessing about my schedule.

You might look at my schedule and say, "But, Richard, maybe the overwhelmed feeling is coming from your life." If you step back from it, you begin to realize that it couldn't be. If it was, then I'd feel overwhelmed all the time—but I don't. I only feel overwhelmed maybe one percent of the time, when instead of doing what's in front of me, I start thinking of everything I must do later that day—or tomorrow, or next week, or in the coming year. In other words, the overwhelmed feeling is present only when I fail to recognize that I'm thinking about it. Once I do, it fades away.

The idea is to recognize your thinking (wake up to the fact that you're doing it) whenever there is a possibility that your own thinking might be getting in your way, making you feel bad or making things seem worse than they are. I received a great letter from a teen who told me that, in the past, she had created a life in her head that included no friends. She'd convinced herself that no one could like her, and that everyone was angry with her. At some moment, after hearing about the importance of recognizing her own thinking, she woke up to the fact that she was simply carrying on in her mind—it was just her thinking.

She went on to say that she still has occasional insecure thoughts about what others are going to think of her, but she has learned to take them a little less seriously. As she recognizes her thinking, the sting of pain leaves her.

So, there you have them—the four pillars of thought—the what, the when, the how, and the fact of. I hope you'll continue to develop a healthy relationship with your own thinking. If you do, your life will be enhanced in many wonderful ways.

# 89

# TAME YOUR ANGER

I don't think it's possible, and it may not even be healthy, to get rid of all your anger. I certainly haven't found a way to do so. Nor would you want to pretend you weren't angry when you are. Yet there is something very comforting about learning to tame your anger, to keep it under control.

When I was eighteen, I was complaining to an adult friend of mine about something that happened to me—I felt I had been cheated out of an award that I had worked very hard to win. I was furious; in fact, I was ranting and raging about the injustice of it all.

My friend said something to me that day that very quickly changed the way I related to my anger. I've spent the last twenty years practicing and remembering what he taught me. Actually, what he said was very simple. In a calm voice he asked me, "Richard, I understand why you are mad. But why *so* mad?"

For a moment, I became quite defensive and fired back, "I'm so mad because it isn't fair!" Again, he responded, "You're right it wasn't fair, and it's okay to be upset, even mad—but why *so* mad? Why are you beating your head against a wall?"

Then it hit me! He was right. I had experienced a disappointment, that was true. It was also true that I may have been cheated, and I certainly had the "right" to be angry. However, in that moment, I also realized that my anger wasn't going to make things better. In fact, it was only going to make things worse. My anger was hurting *me*—after all, I was the one who had to feel it.

It was the first time I was able to see that my anger was coming from *me* and my *own* thoughts—and not from the unfortunate event itself. I felt a freedom that I had never before experienced. It was the feeling that I was, to a large degree, in charge of my emotions. They were coming from inside of me and not from the world.

Imagine hitting your head against a wall and wondering why you had such a bad headache. Then someone came to you and said, "Hey, if you stop banging your head, the pain will stop." In a way, it's the same idea with your anger. If you're thinking about everything that makes you mad, and don't realize that you're the one doing the thinking, you're going to be really, really mad. But once you see that, in fact, you're the one who is thinking all of those angry thoughts, it takes the edge off. It's almost as if you're able to take a step back and create some distance between yourself and whatever it is that you're mad about.

Again, don't get me wrong. You're still going to get angry, and there are plenty of things to be angry about. It's just that, when you recognize where your anger is coming from (your own thoughts), your anger is going to be tamed a little.

Here is one of the most important insights of my life: It's OK to feel angry, but it's also OK not to get carried away with anger and allow it to immobilize me or ruin my life. I hope this insight affects you in a similar way. If it does, it's going to make your life a whole lot less stressful.

# 90

# DON'T BE AN
# APPROVAL-SEEKER

Approval-seekers are people who make the majority of their decisions (at least the important ones) based on what they think other people will think. Rather than following their own conscience, wisdom, intelligence, intuition, and well-thought-out plan, they are more concerned with achieving the approval and acceptance of others—parents, friends, society, or whomever.

Being an approval-seeker creates a number of problems. First and foremost, it saps joy from your life. Making decisions, choosing activities, and working toward your own self-created goals are among the most fulfilling aspects of life. No one can step into your heart and know what it is that you love or what it is you should do. Therefore, although there are exceptions, the fact that someone doesn't understand or disapproves of something you are doing or a decision you are making is usually secondary to what you know to be true in your own life.

Being an approval-seeker also creates an enormous amount of stress and confusion and, ultimately, encourages you to sweat the small stuff. If you're making decisions based primarily on the approval of others, you'll discover that one person will cheer for your decisions and someone else will strongly object or be critical. It's interesting that in certain instances, one person will give you a specific reason why she loves what you are doing—and someone else will use the very same reason to justify why he doesn't like what you're doing. For example, many people have told me, "I love your books because they are simple." Others have told me that they don't like my books because "they are simple." You can't please everyone, and it's not wise to even try. If I tried to please everyone and overcome all objections to the way I do things, I'd go crazy! The only solution is to know that, ultimately, you have to do the very best you can, act as honestly and ethically as possible, and follow your own heart.

Excessive approval-seeking stems from the fear of rejection—the fear that your own decisions aren't good enough. But your decisions *are* good enough because they're yours. Can you imagine how ridiculous it would be if you had to make important decisions for me? You couldn't because you can't get inside my head; only I know what is right for me. It would be just as ridiculous to suggest that I make your decisions for you, or that someone else would be able to do so. We can all be guided and influenced by others—especially by those who love us or who are experts—but ultimately, we must trust ourselves.

Obviously, it's appropriate to get other points of view and to factor those into your decisions. Sometimes you'll discover that other points of view are, indeed, superior to your own, and you may choose to modify something you are doing based on the input you receive from someone else. Further, it's important to understand the distinction between enjoying approval and demanding or requiring it. Everyone loves approval; I sure do. The critical issue is that you don't *have* to have it in order to feel good about yourself or to make independent decisions.

So the issue isn't gathering information, seeking guidance or assistance, being willing to learn and adapt, or preferring approval, but rather it's one of becoming immobilized when others express disapproval.

Becoming less of an approval-seeker is as easy as acknowledging the importance of approval in your life. If you are currently an approval-seeker, the trick is to admit to yourself that this is your tendency. Then, as issues come up and decisions need to be made, step back and ask yourself whether you are making decisions based on what you really want, or whether you are being overly concerned and influenced by the approval factor. Be patient, as this can be a lifelong process. Over time you'll learn to trust your own wisdom and discover the joy and success that comes from doing so. As this happens, you'll be respectful and open to the suggestions from others, but you won't allow their disapproval to stress you out.

## 91

# DON'T BE A
# DISAPPROVAL-SEEKER EITHER

Just as important as being able to live your life without being immobilized by the disapproval of others is the ability to make decisions without being immobilized by the approval of others. I've heard it said that the ultimate sign of maturity is making a decision, even if your parents would approve of it.

Disapproval-seekers are every bit as trapped as approval-seekers. They are people who would never make a decision if they felt that others would approve—especially anyone who was perceived of as a possible authority figure, such as their parents, instructors, or society. These people believe they are being independent, but, in reality, they are imprisoned by their own need to be rebellious.

Years ago I had a funny conversation with a rebellious fifteen-year-old woman. I remembering challenging her to make even one decision that her parents would approve of. I told her I didn't think she could do it. At first she became very defensive and objected to my challenge. But as she started to think about it, she realized that every single decision she made was a decision her parents wouldn't like—the way she dressed, the number of pierced body parts she had, the friends she chose, the activities she focused on, the food she ate, the way she studied (or didn't study), the words she spoke.

It turned out that this particular young woman actually liked what she called "preppy" clothes. She had become so locked into her own self-created persona, however, that she was frightened to admit it. Her freedom came when she realized that she wasn't making decisions based on what she liked, but was burdened by her overwhelming need to make decisions based on what she "knew" her parents would disapprove of. Far from being independent, she was acting like a puppet.

Becoming a disapproval-seeker probably stems from the need to avoid being controlled by others. The problem is, if you take it too far, you *are* being controlled by others. The trick is to learn to make decisions based not on a knee-jerk need to do things differently, but rather from what you honestly and objectively know to be true—for you.

Once you redefine what it means to be free and independent, it's easy to start making adjustments. I remember how difficult it was for me to admit that my parents actually knew quite a bit about life. I only hope that, someday, my kids will realize the same thing about their mother and me.

# 92

# KEEP YOUR SENSE OF HUMOR

One of my favorite quotes comes from the Reverend Henry Ward Beecher. He said, "A person without a sense of humor is like a wagon without springs—jolted by every pebble in the road." I love that quote because, in a way, it speaks to the essence of the don't sweat philosophy. Most of us, at some time, take ourselves and our own personal dramas way too seriously. And when we do, the result is usually pain, fear, and frustration.

Whenever we get into our self-importance mode, we begin to believe that life is all about us. We believe that the things that happen are directed at us and against us. We take things personally. We think about ourselves and our problems too much and become too attached and invested in our opinions. We become totally stubborn, and we lose sight of our humanity and compassion. In a nutshell, we get too serious. All of this feeds into fear, selfishness, doubt, anger, frustration, anxiety, and unhappiness. Indeed, when you're too serious, that's when you sweat the small stuff!

What's more, have you noticed how boring people are when they're too serious and uptight? They're no fun to be around—you feel their heaviness. Sometimes you want to scream out, "Lighten up already!" Do you want to become like that?

With a good sense of humor, our load is lightened. This is particularly true when some of that humor is directed at ourselves. When we can look in the mirror and see that we, too, are a little silly. Our quirks and the little things we attach significance to are just as ridiculous as those of the next person. The actress Ethel Barrymore said, "You grow up the day you have your first laugh—at yourself."

While it's easy to recognize when others are uptight and too serious, it's much harder to see this in ourselves. I'm lucky in that I have two kids who remind me when I fall prey to this ridiculous habit. One will invariably say, "Dad, you've got that serious look again." My older daughter, Jazzy, used to call me "a serious little man."

It's helpful to ask yourself: "Why do I take everything so seriously?" Having a good sense of humor and being able to laugh at yourself doesn't mean you don't care or that you don't try hard. I'm passionate about many things, and I work as hard as anyone I know. I'm happy, however, because I have a good sense of humor. I don't take myself too seriously. I know that a certain number of things are going to go wrong; they always do. Why should I be exempt from what happens to the rest of the world? I know that a certain percentage of people won't like me or will criticize me. I factor that into my assumptions. I know that I will make a lot of mistakes. I don't try to make mistakes, but it's okay with me when I mess up—it means I'm human. I also know that others will make mistakes. I don't always like it, but that's just part of life too.

You have to admit that it's a little funny when people get uptight about little stupid things. The advantage I have is that I think it's funny when I do; I see myself as a character. If you can see the humor in life, you're going to enjoy most of it. You'll have more patience, acceptance, and perspective than most others. These feelings will enhance your joy and will keep you from burning out.

Humor is an interesting topic because, when you suggest to people that they take themselves less seriously, they often believe you are minimizing their troubles and frustrations. Of course, you are not. The truth is, we have many troubles, some of which are very serious. Life can be very hard and very painful. Yet a sense of humor helps us to keep those dramas in perspective. It makes life interesting and fun during easy times, and assists us when the going gets tough.

I hope in the midst of all the serious stuff around, you can maintain and develop a good sense of humor. It will serve you well.

# 93

# ADMIT THAT YOU'RE WRONG—
# OR THAT YOU'VE MADE A MISTAKE

One of my favorite questions I've ever been asked came from a thirteen-year-old girl during a book-signing event. She asked, "What in the world does admitting you're wrong or admitting your mistakes have to do with not sweating the small stuff?" Luckily, I had an answer.

Consider, for a moment, all the energy we spend defending ourselves and proving our positions when someone thinks we're wrong. Think about all the arguing, correcting, and trying to get people to see our innocence or our rationale for doing something. Consider the pressure associated with having to convince people we are right when they think we are wrong, or the stress of having to change someone's point of view. Think of the hundreds of times we've had to explain ourselves—our reasons and justifications for our actions—when someone accuses us of making a mistake. If that doesn't cause one to "sweat," what does?

Now imagine how much easier your life would be if you could eliminate a good percentage of all that. Wouldn't it be a relief when you *are* wrong or when you *do* make a mistake, if, rather than compounding the stress for additional hours, days, or weeks by constantly having to think about it and defend yourself, the issue were to fade away, resolve itself, and you could get on with your life?

The way to make that happen is to make the decision that, when you are wrong or when you do make a mistake, you admit it. Doing so defuses the situation, taking some of the "charge" away.

I was running late to pick up my daughter and was driving too fast. I knew it too. A police officer pulled me over and began giving me a lecture as he was about to write the ticket. Rather than defend my actions, I admitted I was wrong and said that I was sorry and that I deserved the ticket. I was sincere and I was not trying to manipulate him.

He asked me why I was driving too fast. I told him that, while it was not a very good excuse, I was running late to pick up my daughter. He responded, "But that is a reason to be concerned." I agreed but said, "It would be, but she is in good hands and is in no danger. I shouldn't have been driving so fast." He was so impressed by my willingness to admit my mistake that he decided against writing the ticket.

I'm not suggesting that the same explanation would get me out of another ticket. It probably wouldn't. In fact, I did deserve the ticket. What I'm suggesting is that human beings, all of us, have a need to be right. The police officer who let me off the hook appreciated the fact that I had allowed him to be right, without forcing him to express his authority.

The same dynamic applies in all day-to-day living. If someone says to you, for example, "You weren't listening to me," and you weren't, you'd be so much better off simply admitting it. You might say, "You know, you're right. I wasn't listening. I'm sorry, and I'll try to listen better from now on." At that point, it's over. The very person who has accused you of doing something wrong is probably now on your side, thinking of you as the "good guy." The situation is resolved, the stress is over. You move forward.

Compare that to arguing with the person or defending yourself by saying, "I was too listening!" Think about your odds of changing the person's mind—not very good. She is convinced you weren't listening. In her mind she is certain she is right. To argue, fight back, disagree, or launch a counterattack is only going to compound the problem and create additional stress.

Obviously, if the person is completely off base or if you're certain you've not made a mistake and you're not wrong, there's no reason to admit to guilt. But if your goal is less stress and an easier life, a little humility goes a long way.

## 94

# REMEMBER THAT EVERYONE
# HAS THE RIGHT TO BE HAPPY

Someone once asked me, "If you were to single out a phrase or saying that has helped you to keep your perspective during times you might otherwise be annoyed with others, what would it be?" The words that came out of my mouth were, "Everyone has the right to be happy."

Think about it for a minute. Everyone *wants* to be happy—people you know and those you don't; people you like as well as people you can't stand. Good people, bad people—everyone wants to be happy and everyone, in his or her own way, is trying to be happy. Even people who do bad things often are doing those bad things in some weird attempt to make themselves happier. It's just part of being human.

When you factor this knowledge into your life, it's amazing what can happen to you. Rather than being upset or bothered by people when they say or do things that you wish they wouldn't, you're able to keep your perspective and sense of humor while remaining compassionate.

I asked Rachel, a sixteen-year-old, if she could apply this wisdom to her life. After only a few seconds of thought, it hit her. She said that a few days earlier she had become furious with a friend who was bragging about her new clothes and her boyfriend. She said that she hated it when people bragged or acted self-centered.

For the first time in her life, however, she could see what has happening in a new way. All of a sudden, she understood that her friend, like everyone else, acted this way simply because she wanted to be happy. For whatever reason, her friend felt that showing off or bragging made her feel better about herself. And although Rachel still felt she could "do without the attitude," she did see the bigger picture. Despite how annoying it was, she could see the innocence in her friend's behavior. Her anger softened, and she even smiled as she said to me, "Well, you know, she really does have the right to be happy. I don't think that's the best way to go about it—but she does have the right."

While Rachel certainly would prefer that her friend would act differently, she did feel compassion for her friend for feeling the need to be that way. As you think about it, you'll see that the same thing applies to practically anything else you're feeling annoyed or bothered by. I'm certainly not suggesting that you excuse all negative behavior, but remembering that everyone has a right to be happy does provide a "mental shield" against taking things too seriously.

The next time someone does something that bugs you, rather than reacting as usual, see if you can remember that everyone has the right to be happy. You might find yourself free from irritation for the very first time.

# 95

# GO WITH THE FLOW

It seems to me that almost everyone is familiar with this phrase, but that almost no one adheres to its wisdom. This is sad because, far from being nothing more than a catchy phrase, "Going with the flow" is actually a powerful way to keep your stress under control.

One of the problems with being rigid and uptight is that day-to-day life isn't static. Instead, it's a constantly changing and evolving process. It's a flow of activity. If you go with the flow, without too much resistance, your life will be like a graceful dance. You'll be moving forward but making constant adjustments. On the other hand, if you resist the flow, or go against it, your life will be more like a battleground, a constant struggle and source of frustration. Rather than making graceful and appropriate adjustments, you'll be bumping up against resistance and trying to force things to go right. The only time you'll experience peace is when everything is going just right—and, realistically, how often does that happen?

In a way, life is like a giant web. Thousands and thousands of things are happening and interacting with one another. You're catching people in bad moods, plans get altered, someone is upset with you, mistakes are inevitable, there is chaos. Some things turn out well, others don't. To go with the flow means that you accept the fact that life is somewhat chaotic and that there are many things over which we have little or no control. Rather than resist each event that doesn't go your way, instead, choose to respond with acceptance. It means you do all you can to put the odds in your favor, yet you are okay when they aren't. Rather than fighting life, you embrace it.

A group of teenage girls was waiting in line to see a movie. When they finally got to the ticket counter, after a long wait, they were informed that the movie was sold out. While almost everyone in the line behind them began freaking out, one of the teens calmly gathered her friends and said, "Don't worry about it—we'll find something else to do."

That was it. No drama, no threats to management, no complaints, and no huffing and puffing. Most of all, she was experiencing no stress. Did she care? You bet she did. But was there anything she could do about it? No way. The way she handled it, I had no doubt in my mind that the young women were going to have fun anyway, regardless of the sudden and disappointing change of plans. Jointly, they were demonstrating their ability to go with the flow and to not sweat the small stuff.

What I found most interesting about the scene was that almost everyone else in the very same line was bent out of shape, angry, and frustrated. You could tell that their entire evening was going to be adversely affected because they simply did not know how to go with the flow. My guess is that most of the people in line were experienced moviegoers. And I'll bet that nineteen times out of twenty, everything goes smoothly and they get to see their movie of choice. Yet when "real life" happens and something goes awry, the typical reaction is to become overly dramatic and disappointed.

I could share hundreds of similar stories where most of the people involved stress out and overreact over some little thing. All the stories have a common denominator: the inability to go with the flow and the inability to not take minor disappointments too seriously. This unaccepting attitude leads to almost constant frustration, feelings of disappointment, irritation, bother, and stress. In addition, people who can't go with the flow are a drag to be around because you can sense their tension.

This is a topic worth thinking about because not only are there incredible benefits from going with the flow, but it's pretty easy to learn. What's required is a willingness to keep reminding yourself that most things we get upset about aren't quite as critical as we make them out to be. Remind yourself that there are always going to be inconveniences and hassles to deal with. That's just part of life, and it's OK that it's that way. As you begin to convince yourself of this truth, and as you become more accepting of it, you'll be on your way to a happier and more peaceful life.

## 96

# EXPERIENCE
# DELAYED REACTIONS

I'd guess that a huge percentage of fights, conflicts, arguments, and other stressful encounters could be avoided if more people would learn to experience delayed reactions. A "delayed reaction" is simply an intentional hesitation that you make between the time something happens and the time you react. It's creating a space between your initial feelings of irritation and the time you act on that irritation.

A delayed reaction is the opposite of a knee-jerk reaction. A knee-jerk reaction, as you know, is like an automatic response. It's an instant (usually negative) reaction to some type of stimulus. For example, someone calls you a name or criticizes you, and you immediately fly off the handle. You get some bad news, and without so much as taking a breath, you panic. Or you see your boyfriend talking to another girl and you freak out. The point is, it's instant—almost as if something else has taken over. There is no space; just a quick reaction. You've probably already realized that a staggering percentage of instant reactions backfire and end up hurting us as well as everyone else involved.

It's fascinating, however, to observe how quickly the intensity of anger, fear, or other emotions fade away if you hold off on your reaction—give it a minute to settle, take a deep breath, give it some space. You'll notice that something that seems terrible one minute often seems slightly less terrible the next. Or something that makes you see red one moment will be only slightly irritating the next.

This is great to know, because what it tells us is that if something is making us really angry (or sad, frustrated, stressed, anxious) right now, it probably won't seem so bad in a short while. And, awhile after that, it won't seem even that bad. So the question becomes: If something isn't going to seem so bad in a little while, what's the point of overreacting right now? Why yell and scream and get all frustrated and stressed if those feelings are going to fade away anyway? Why risk telling someone off in a moment of rage when, in all likelihood, you'll feel less rage five minutes later?

In *Don't Sweat the Small Stuff*, I included a strategy entitled "Ask Yourself the Question, 'Will This Matter a Year from Now?'" Obviously, some things *will* matter a year from now. Yet most things won't. The trick is to learn which things are really critical and which things are pretty much "small stuff." It's the small stuff that you don't want to waste your energy on.

Think about all the fights you've seen and the reactive statements that have hurt someone's feelings. Think about how many lives have been ruined or hurt—and how many people are in jail—simply because someone couldn't keep from having a dangerous knee-jerk reaction.

Imagine, for a moment, what would have happened had the person inflicting the harsh words or the fist simply hesitated, taken a deep breath, and experienced a delayed reaction. The world still wouldn't be perfect, but it sure would be quite a bit more peaceful.

# 97

# KEEP IN MIND THAT AS ONE DOOR CLOSES, ANOTHER ONE OPENS

One of the greatest sources of stress, sadness, and frustration for many of us is when we feel that a door has closed, as if a chapter in our life is over. We can feel sadness, loss, grief, and, perhaps most of all, fear of the unknown.

Some of the most common instances of this source of stress are when you break up with a boyfriend or girlfriend or when you move to a new town. You sense that your life will never be the same, and fear that it won't be as good. Similar feelings can come up when, for any number of reasons, you lose a friend or when you move on to a new school, leaving friends and memories behind. The same can be true when you complete something you've worked hard on and that you have enjoyed; it's now over and the need, desire, or opportunity to continue no longer exists.

A comforting truth of life to keep in mind is that as one door closes, another one, by definition, opens in response. It doesn't always seem that way immediately, but it's helpful to know that it's true. And embracing this understanding makes changes, transitions, even disappointments much easier to deal with.

It's strange to think about, but had your parents not broken up with all of their previous "serious" relationships with the opposite sex, you wouldn't be here today! By breaking off previous relationships, it opened the door for your parents to be together—and for you to be born.

In the same way, you probably had friends who moved, went on to new schools, or decided not be your friend anymore. And, painful as it may have been, the act of them no longer being such an important part of your life created the time, need, and energy for you to create new, special friendships. Likewise, if you don't make the cheerleading squad, football team, or anything else you were hoping for, it paves the way for other doors to open. This is not a "pretend everything's all right" philosophy, but rather an honest look at the way life really works. The more you reflect on this idea, the more sense it will make.

This philosophy has helped me through many periods of transition as well as many disappointments in my life, helping me find peace. As a teen, I was a champion tennis player, having practiced hard, almost every day, for many years. When it was time to give it up and move on to something else, the knowledge that new doors would open made the changes in my life much easier to embrace. Rather than regret or sadness, my primary feelings were enthusiasm for what might be next. Had I continued my tennis career rather than following my heart, I doubt I would be writing this book today.

I encourage you to give this idea some serious thought. Think back to how many times in your life you've ended something, only to begin something even better—and how necessary it is that things come to an end. The trick is to use this same philosophy in the midst of a transition. If you do, you'll find yourself moving through your life with far less struggle.

# 98

# EMBRACE THE ATTITUDE, "THIS TOO SHALL PASS"

You may have heard the phrase "This too shall pass." It's not just a saying that sounds good in theory. Rather, it's a phrase worth looking at because if you can embrace it, your day-to-day life will be much easier and less stressful. You also will be able to get through difficult times more gracefully.

It's been said that the only certainty in life is change. Every day that has ever started has ended. No experience lasts forever. Each thought you've ever had is over. So is every breath. We are born, we grow up, we get older. Life is always changing.

You were an infant, now you're a teen. I was a teen, now I'm almost forty. A school year begins and it ends. We have hardships and they are resolved. You get the flu and then you're fine. You break your arm, it heals. Something is popular, until it fades. It always does. Music that was "in" five years ago is hardly remembered. You're sure today's music will be popular forever, but it won't be. People fall in love and say, "This feeling will never end," but it changes. You're so embarrassed that you can't show your face, and you think the feeling will last forever. A few days later the embarrassment is totally forgotten and nobody cares. Someone is furious at you—or you at him—until it changes and you're back together, as if it had never happened.

A team wins the World Series or the Super Bowl, and the fans go wild. The very next year, the same team finishes last. You've been in thousands of low moods, and they all went away. You've been in great moods too—but eventually they went back down. There are no exceptions. Indeed, everything passes.

You can take great comfort in knowing that everything passes. Since there are no exceptions—none—it means that if you are sad, you won't always be sad. If you're angry, the anger will fade. If you fail, you'll bounce back. If someone has hurt you, that feeling will change. If you lose a love, there will be another. Indeed, there is something very reassuring in knowing that, whatever it is, however hard it seems, it too will pass. You can count on it.

My dear friend Robert and his terrific girlfriend were killed by a drunken driver while driving to my wedding. It was the most painful experience that I had ever been through. I almost had to postpone the wedding. I cried all night and thought the pain would never end. And while, to this day, I still miss him (and say hi to his photo), the pain has long turned to gratitude. I feel fortunate to have known him and to be able to call him my friend. What helped me to get through my pain was the hope that even that amount of pain would eventually go away. This too shall pass, I was told. And it did.

I've since learned to trust this wisdom in all aspects of life. It's a very practical attitude to embrace. When you are absolutely certain that everything will pass, it is much easier to let go of things, especially "small stuff." This perspective allows you to know that everything will be okay. It gives you hope and confidence that things aren't as bad as they seem. It makes forgiving and maintaining a sense of humor easier. It helps you to stop sweating the small stuff. Nothing is as aggravating, painful, or difficult when you know that it's not forever.

Rest assured that whatever you're going through, big or small, it too shall pass.

# 99

# LISTEN TO THOSE
# WAKE-UP CALLS

As I look back on my teens and on my whole life thus far, it's clear that I received a number of important wake-up calls. As I inquire into the lives of others, most people feel the same way. Many will acknowledge that the wake-up calls are there for the taking, as long as we acknowledge and respect them.

Wake-up calls can be anything from a fight with your sibling that gets a little out of hand or a little too rough, to being caught cheating on a test and thrown out of school. In both of these instances, and in so many others like them, the experience sends a shock, minor or major, through your mind, a feeling like, "Oh, no, what have I done?" You might feel awkward or embarrassed—or you might feel uncomfortable or relieved. In any event, there is a message to be heard.

While you usually don't enjoy or appreciate wake-up calls while they are happening, often you may look back on these experiences as being turning points in your life; extremely important lessons that were learned. I heard a story of a teen who was caught stealing. It was humiliating, embarrassing, and painful. Yet that teen grew up to be a kind, generous, and loving person, someone who has really made a difference in the lives of others. When asked, he points to that awful experience as being among the most important in his entire life. It turned out not to be a tragedy after all because he learned so much from it.

Two things can happen after a mess-up, mistake, or mishap. You can pretend it didn't happen, deny your involvement, run away, or avoid the consequences the best you can. Or you can say to yourself and others, "I'm going to learn from this experience and become a better person because of it." This decision is one of those really difficult things to make in life, but one that makes an enormous difference over the long run.

Recently someone asked me what I believed were some of the keys to surviving the teen years. My answer was that it's tough to say, but that listening to the wake-up calls was certainly up near the top of the list. I believe this is true because every one of us makes mistakes. There isn't a person alive today who hasn't, and if someone tells you otherwise, she's lying or fooling herself. So the only remaining question becomes, "What are you going to do with those mistakes?" Will you listen to what they are trying to teach you—or not? I hope you'll take this one to heart and tuck it away for future reference.

# 100

# CONTINUE YOUR JOURNEY

The hardest part of writing this book was deciding where to end. I'm hoping that this book has been a source of inspiration. I hope it was helpful and useful, and that you really take it to heart. If possible, reread it and try to put the strategies into practice in your life.

You probably can sense from my writing style and content that I'm a true optimist. I believe that anyone reading this book has the capacity to become kinder, gentler, happier, wiser, and more productive. I hope you sense that you don't have to make giant changes overnight to become a less stressed person. It's not a contest, and you don't have to make a big deal out of it. Instead, focus on little things: a change here, another one there. Pretty soon, it all starts to add up. Some people read my books and say, "I can do that—that's easy." And they're right. So they make a tiny change, a shift in attitude or behavior. And, lo and behold, it works. They feel a little happier or less stressed, or they resolve a conflict a little more easily, or they reach out to someone. So they continue to make more changes.

If you've learned some new things or received any insights, or if your life has been touched in any positive way, I urge you to continue your journey. Read other books designed to improve the quality of your life. Hang out with happy people. Take classes that can teach you new ways of being in the world. Get involved in your community and/or your church. Become more generous and forgiving. Be spiritual. Make kindness, compassion, generosity, and happiness important priorities in your life. If you'd like, write to me at my Web site (www.dontsweat.com) and tell me what you're doing. I'd love to hear from you. Spend your time wisely because the way you spend your moments today will determine the quality of your life tomorrow.

Don't make the conclusion of this book an ending; instead, make it a beginning. By becoming happier and learning not to sweat the small stuff, you not only help yourself, but you become an instrument to help the world at large. You literally become part of the solution. After all, when you have what you want and need emotionally, your natural instinct will be to reach out to others. That is my highest hope.

It may sound corny, but I'm going to say it anyway. You are our future. You can and do make a difference. You are important, and you have the capacity to learn to not sweat the small stuff. I send you my love and best wishes.

Treasure the gift of life.